BY THE SAME AUTHOR

*Treasure in the Thames*

# *GREAT MOMENTS IN*
# ARCHAEOLOGY

---

The Great Moments series gives vivid and exciting accounts of some of the most dramatic incidents in the story of man's achievements—in mountaineering, in sport, in flying, in exploration, and in many other kinds of adventure. They are true stories, about some of the world's most determined and courageous men and women.

PUBLISHED

Great Moments in

*Mountaineering : Sport : Flying : Exploration*

*Sea : Archaeology*

IN PREPARATION

Great Moments in

*Music : Theatre : Motoring : Detection : Railways*

*Medicine : Pioneers : Engineering*

# *Great Moments in* ARCHAEOLOGY

*IVOR NOËL HUME*

ILLUSTRATED
BY BRUCE CORNWELL

PHOENIX HOUSE LTD · LONDON
ROY PUBLISHERS · NEW YORK

Printed in Great Britain
in 11-point Monotype Baskerville by
C. Tinling & Co., Ltd., Liverpool, London and Prescot for
Phoenix House Ltd., 38 William IV Street, Charing Cross, W.C.2
and Roy Publishers, 30 East 74th Street, New York 21, N.Y.

*Library of Congress*
*Catalog Card Number 58-5383*

CONTENTS

## ILLUSTRATIONS

# ACKNOWLEDGMENTS

The author and publishers wish to express their gratitude to the following for permission to quote from the named books:

To Cassell & Co., publishers of *The Tomb of Tutankhamen* by Howard Carter; to Messrs Harper Brothers for *The Silent World* by Commander J. Y. Cousteau, and for *Ilios, City and Country of the Trojans* by Heinrich Schliemann; and finally to the Houghton Mifflin Co. for extracts from *People of the Serpent* by Edward Herbert Thompson.

## *CHAPTER ONE*

# PICTURES IN THE DARK

On the morning of the 12 September 1940, the Battle of Britain was at its height. The Kentish sky was being torn by exploding shells and scored by vapour trails and the black, spiralling smoke of plunging aircraft. But in Vichy France the sun shone out of a silent heaven and in the small town of Montignac five boys were wondering how best to pass the day. Eventually, after much argument, they decided to go off into the hills with their sporting guns.

Montignac lies in the valley of the River Vézère in the Dordogne department of France. On either side of the valley rise walls of craggy hills, some of them topped by mediaeval, turreted castles which stand, wreathed in a pale haze, like scenery from a pantomime. On this September day the five boys were destined to live through an adventure more astonishing than anything that the stage could offer. Their names were Ravidat—he was seventeen and the oldest—Marcal, Quéroy, Estréguil, and Coencas. The last two were refugees from German-occupied France, but the others were local boys who had known the hills and dales all their lives. Together they set out, with two guns between them, and accompanied by their scruffy mongrel dog whose name was Robot.

In fine high spirits they made their way out of the town and up the valley towards the wooded hills where they hoped to find the best sport. Robot bounded on ahead wagging his tail and yelping with the sheer joy of living. On they all went, upwards over the vine-covered slopes towards the ruined building known as the Château de Lascaux. It was never an imposing structure. Indeed, the only noble thing about it was its name. This was no romantic mediaeval castle, merely a large house built two hundred years ago by a local clergyman. The name would suggest that it was the manor house of the village of Lascaux; but actually there is no such place. The château is a ruin not because it was sacked during the French Revolution or was burnt in some dramatic fire, but because it was simply never finished. Until Ravidat and his four friends set out on that fateful morning Lascaux meant nothing more than an unhappy memorial to a foolish man.

The land which belonged to the château lies on the side of a hill which has been eroded almost smooth by the passing of time. The soil which thinly hides the limestone rock is poor and will support only spindly birches, firs, and hazels, with here and there a stunted oak. Some forty years ago a particularly severe storm had torn one of the fir trees out of the ground leaving an unusually large hole. Peasants from nearby villages who had grazing rights on the Lascaux acres had tried to fill this hole. But try as they did, they were never very successful. However well they did the job, it would only need a little heavy rain to open the hole up again. They therefore decided to build a fence round the opening; but even this did not prevent an unfortunate donkey from falling down it. The poor creature died before anyone discovered where it had gone and thereafter the hole became known as the 'Donkey's Dip'.

Ravidat and his friends had been amusing themselves amid the château ruins when they suddenly noticed that Robot, the dog, was no longer with them. They called and shouted; but they heard no answering yelp. Then one of the lads remembered the 'Dip'. Quickly they pushed their way through the scrub which surrounded the hole, and they were soon standing at the lip, looking down into the rubble-strewn opening. A scree of pebbles and limestone chips stretched diagonally downwards until it disappeared into the shadows of the overhanging stones.

Ravidat lay down at the mouth and shouted into the darkness. His voice boomed away as though into a giant funnel, echoing and re-echoing down into the bowels of the earth. The boys waited in silence, their ears strained to catch an answering bark. But none came. They looked at each other and shrugged. Robot, they decided, was not there. Then, just as they were debating where they should look next, a frightened yelp came out of the hole. Ravidat sighed with relief. The little dog was found. But almost at once relief turned to dismay, for it was one thing to locate the animal but quite another to rescue it.

First they selected a round stone and rolled it down the slope into the entrance. The boys listened intently as they heard it rattling away into the distance, finally dropping with a thud onto they knew not what. The partially blocked opening was much too small to permit even the youngest of the lads to wriggle through, and their only tools were a knife and five pairs of bare hands. But encouraged by Robot's yelps, they set about pulling first one stone and then another away from the entrance. Sticks cut from nearby trees were used as levers and before long the hole was large enough for Ravidat to slide through. He eased himself into the opening feet first, with his hands supported by his friends. But in a few seconds they could no longer reach him and he was alone in the darkness. The rubble scree sloped ever downwards. As he edged his way along, he expected that at any moment his feet would reach the brink of a sheer drop. But nothing happened. Suddenly, instead of the expected void, his groping foot sank into dry sand. He had reached the bottom. As Ravidat looked up, he realized that he had not slid nearly as far as it had seemed, for he could clearly see his friends' anxious faces as they peered into the darkness only 25 feet or so above him.

The boy quickly lit a match and to his relief he soon found the dog, shaken but with no bones broken. Once satisfied on this score, Ravidat had time to look round him. A few matches held aloft and thrown, burning, into the

With matches held high, they gingerly made their way forward.

darkness soon showed that he was in no immediate danger of plunging into an abyss.

'I'm in a cave,' Ravidat shouted to his friends. 'Come on down. I'm going to see where it goes!'

The four boys needed no second bidding. This was just the sort of adventure that they had been wanting. Once assembled on the sandy cave floor, they paused to get accustomed to the darkness and then, with matches held high, they gingerly made their way forward. They soon found that they were in a single rock chamber about 30 feet wide and 60 feet in length. Above them the roof rose upwards into a water-worn dome, not smooth-faced, but etched out in a series of folds and whorls like petrified storm clouds.

Suddenly Ravidat cried out excitedly, 'Hey, Marcal, look there! Look over there!'

As they stared in the direction of Ravidat's pointing match, the light from their own small flames cast a dwindling, yellow glow onto the wall of the cavern. The boys were suddenly surrounded, it seemed, by a host of prancing, racing, charging, and leaping animals—not live animals, but creatures painted on the walls and roof of the cave. Here were strange, long-bodied oxen and thick-coated bison, and there stags with massive, waving antlers, thick-necked horses, and small, Disney-like ponies. Wherever they looked there were animals, some outlined in black and washed in with browns, yellows, reds, and mauves, while others were drawn as simple black silhouettes.

Ravidat and his friends were amazed and excited. It was as though they had stumbled into some subterranean picture gallery; but here the paintings were more dramatic than oil colour on canvas could ever be, for many of the animals were painted on and sometimes covered by a thin stalactitic film which had collected through the centuries and made them glisten as though they had been drawn on glass. Long before the boys could absorb the wonder of it all, the last match had burnt down to the fingers and the show was over. Then, almost too astounded to speak, they made their way back towards the entrance and out into the September sunlight.

Not one of the boys had any knowledge of archaeology. But they were convinced that the paintings were of great age, and they were equally certain that if news of their discovery leaked out they would quickly lose control of what they considered to be *their* cave. They resolved, therefore, to say not a word to anyone. Bursting with excitement though they were, the boys steadfastly resisted the temptation to share the secret even with their parents. On each of the next five days the friends went out on their 'hunting expeditions', but now they were armed with lights instead of guns, and with every trip they penetrated further and further into the Lascaux cave.

The main chamber into which Ravidat had slid proved to dwindle to a narrow passage which soon disappeared into a crevice in the rock face. But at the entrance to this passage another branched away to the right which, in its turn, became T-shaped and split into two small chambers. The left of these is now known as the 'Nave' and this, too, shrinks to a narrow passage which finally loses itself in a crack in the rock. The right-hand cave, the 'Apse,' has no tailing passage, but ends in a fissure in the floor which drops some 30 feet into a final chamber called the 'Crypt'. That also has a passage running away from it, but this is blocked by debris from its collapsed roof. Animal paintings have been found in all save one of these chambers and passages. By the end of the week, the boys had explored all the caves that they could reach. They then agreed that there was nothing more to be gained by remaining silent and so they resolved to reveal their secret to M. Léon Laval, the local schoolmaster.

As Ravidat and his friends told their story, their description of the animals sounded so fantastic that the master suspected that he was being made the victim of a practical joke. But although he was still unconvinced, M. Laval agreed to go and look for himself. By the time he had puffed up the hillside and had scrambled through the narrow opening into the cave, the poor man was ready to tell the boys exactly what he thought of practical jokers. But no sooner were the torches flashed onto the walls than his doubts vanished.

The Dordogne is world-famous as a source of relics of prehistoric man, and there can be few Frenchmen living there who do not profess some knowledge of these matters. M. Laval was no expert but he probably knew more than most. He therefore had no hesitation in proclaiming the paintings to be a sensational discovery. But he was not prepared to answer the boys' questions about their age. This was a matter for an expert, he announced.

Once back in Montignac, the schoolmaster told the story to a M. Maurice Thaon who, in turn, informed the great French archaeologist the Abbé Breuil. So it was that only nine days after Ravidat had first slid into the cavern in search of his dog, a group of France's most eminent archaeologists arrived at the brink of the 'Donkey's Dip'. It took them but a few minutes to realize that the schoolmaster had been right. This *was* a major discovery. Indeed, many experts were to describe the paintings as the finest of their kind ever found in France, and equalled nowhere in Europe except, perhaps, at Altamira in northern Spain.

News of the discovery spread like wildfire, and before long everyone in the district was considering the cave as a tourist attraction and wondering how best to exploit it. The experts, on the other hand, were not interested in such matters, and they decided that the cave should not yet be opened to the public.

All through the war years experts continued their work of recording and photographing the dozens of individual paintings. A massive wall was built across the entrance to the first chamber through which the experts, and later the tourists, could pass into the main gallery. Electric lighting was installed so that the paintings would be shown to their greatest advantage, enabling them to be seen a hundred times better than they had been by the artists who painted them.

The experts were all agreed that the Lascaux paintings belonged to the oldest phase of human art and that, of their date, they are the finest yet discovered. Why, we ask, did those artists of twenty-five thousand to thirty thousand years ago take such astonishing trouble to decorate the walls of caverns which would never see the light of day? At best, their work would be seen by the smoky, flickering flame of burning tallow in a limestone lamp. Did they do it just for the fun of it or was there some specific purpose for the paintings?

The experts believe that most of the painted caves (and there are others in the same district) were meeting-places where magical rites were performed. Broadly speaking, we may call them temples, although we know nothing of any individual gods who might have been worshipped there. It is generally believed that men gathered in these caves to indulge in rituals which they thought would bring them luck in their hunting. This would account for the fact that nearly all the paintings are of animals which Old Stone Age or Paleolithic people would have killed for food.

In some of the paintings the ancient artists have shown feathered barbs being shot at the beasts, while in others the animals are seen with arrows or spears protruding from their flanks. In one scene a large black cow is depicted jumping towards a curious, purplish-red object looking rather like a barred gate, but which some authorities believe to be a trap.

One of the many astonishing features of the Lascaux paintings is the fact that the artists were so sure of themselves. These were not raw amateurs doodling on the walls of their caves in a tortuous attempt to teach themselves to draw. They already knew what they wanted and they knew how best to achieve it. They understood the problems of perspective and they were even able to make use of the curves, fissures, and undulations of the rocks so as to

The story picture in the cave known as the 'Crypt'

achieve a feeling of depth. The methods of drawing the outlines and of applying the colours illustrate the artists' command of differing techniques.

It is clear that the paintings were not all created at any one time. On the contrary, they were added to over a long period, later examples sometimes being drawn on top of the old. It has been estimated that the artists were at work in the Lascaux caverns for some ten thousand years. The earliest creation is the stencilled hand and arm of a child. This was achieved by a child pressing his or her arm against the wetted rock while someone else blew red pigment round it. Then, when the arm was removed, the outline remained. This, to many people, is one of the most fascinating of all the Lascaux pictures. Who can resist the temptation to wonder who the child was and what he or she was thinking while standing there in the gloomy cavern all those thousands of years ago?

Today, all the Lascaux chambers are open to the public—all save one. The exception is the 'Crypt', which is unfortunately too difficult for the average person to reach. In it there is only a single, comparatively small, painted scene. But it is one of the more interesting, even though it is probably the most recent, having been painted little more than fifteen thousand years ago. Whereas the majority of the pictures in the main galleries are of single animals, the scene in the 'Crypt' tells a definite story.

The picture has come to be known as the 'Prehistoric Tragedy', or sometimes simply as 'The Scene'. Various attempts have been made to interpret the action of the story; but we shall never know which, if any, of them is correct. On the right of the group a great, shaggy-maned bison has been speared by a javelin. But the animal, dangerous even at the point of death, has gored and slain the hunter. The man is drawn only in outline with 'pin-man' arms and legs, and with only four digits on each hand. His head, too, is a little odd; but it is thought that he is wearing a bird-like mask. This little man had apparently set out on his hunting expedition carrying his spear, his spear-thrower, and his magical staff topped with the figure of a bird. In the painting the luckless huntsman is toppling rigidly backwards, while his spear-thrower and magic staff have fallen from his lifeless hand.

The vengeance of the dying bison was not the end of the 'Prehistoric Tragedy', for to the left of the dead hunter a massive woolly rhinoceros is seen ambling stolidly away. What role, people ask, did the rhino play in this unhappy tale? The answer is possibly to be found in the drawing of the bison, for the artist has shown it to have been badly gouged, an injury far greater than could have been caused by the hunter's spear. The suggestion is that after killing the man, the wounded bison was set upon by the rhinoceros and ripped by its murderous horns.

If this is a true interpretation of the 'Prehistoric Tragedy', we may well wonder whether it is not in fact a record of something which really happened. The Abbé

Breuil has even suggested that the body of the dead hunter may have been buried in the 'Crypt' and that the painting was intended as a memorial to him.

Today Lascaux has become a Mecca for archaeologists and tourists from all over the world—thanks to Marcal, Quéroy, Coencas, Estréguil, Ravidat, and most of all to Robot, the little mongrel dog. Alas, Robot is no more, and of the now grown-up boys, only two remain in Montignac. It would have made a better ending to the story to have told how the five boys were handsomely rewarded and how they were able to live happily ever after. But although Montignac waxes fat on the tourist trade which their discovery has brought it, the boys received nothing. Ravidat and Marcal, however, were given jobs as custodians and guides at Lascaux, so that every day during the tourist season they are to be seen telling their story over and over again. We might think that this would be more of a punishment than a reward for having made one of the world's greatest prehistoric discoveries.

## CHAPTER TWO

# THE ROYAL CEMETERY AT UR

In the bleak, forbidding desert to the south of the river Euphrates and midway between Baghdad and the Persian Gulf rise a series of sand-covered mounds. These are all that remain of the fabulous Biblical city of Ur—the birthplace of Abraham. The tallest and largest of the mounds was briefly investigated as long ago as 1854, and it was then that inscribed tablets were found which identified the site by name. Nothing more was done until the end of the century, when an American expedition visited the area, but achieved little from the project. A party of British archaeologists carried out more rewarding excavations during the first World War; but lack of funds prevented their work from continuing. Nevertheless, the results of this excavation encouraged the University of Pennsylvania to join with the British Museum in 1922 in mounting a new expedition which was to be led by the well-known British archaeologist Leonard Woolley. This great figure was not then at the peak of his career and was still to be knighted, but he was already universally admired and respected in archaeological circles. His excavations at Ur were destined to be his crowning achievement.

The world's great artistic achievements are naturally admired by experts and laymen alike. But many people forget that the history of art does not begin in classical times, but extends back along the long, dusty road of evolution, through the civilizations of the Hittites, the Phoenicians, the Minoans, of Babylon and Egypt. Far behind them we find the Sumerians—the inhabitants of the desert city of Ur, who flourished more than five thousand years ago.

Leonard Woolley's excavations began in the normal manner with a series of exploratory trenches, some of which exposed stretches of the city wall and beyond it part of a huge dump of domestic rubbish which had been thrown over the wall and allowed to pile up outside. This accumulation proved to be at least 40 feet in thickness, indicating that that particular form of refuse disposal had been popular for a very long time. Cutting into the rubbish the excavators came upon a large number of graves in which the mortal remains of the citizens were interred. Some were wrapped in matting held in place by long copper pins, while others lay in coffins of wood, basketwork, or clay. Each grave contained its quota of funerary pots as well as the trinkets and prized possessions of the dead person; but unfortunately many of these graves proved to have been disturbed and robbed of their valuables by grave-diggers when digging shafts for later burials. The archaeologists found that the process of digging graves and throwing out rubbish went on at one and the same time, for the earlier graves were completely sealed by later rubbish, which in its turn was cut into by subsequent grave-digging. The presence of all these burials with their accompanying grave-gods provided Leonard Woolley with ideal dating evidence for the different layers of rubbish and, indeed, for the dating of the city itself.

The discovery and excavation of the citizens' cemetery could not in its own right claim to be one of the great moments in archaeology. But there was more to come. Towards the end of the 1926-7 season the diggers came upon the mouth of a large, loosely filled pit which, when excavated, revealed what appeared to be a floor made from blocks and slabs of limestone. This discovery posed an interesting problem, for there were no stones to be found in the Euphrates valley and to obtain these massive pieces it would have been necessary to have brought them from quarries at least thirty miles away in the higher desert. Why then should so much trouble have been taken merely to make a floor for a pit? The question was still unanswered when the arrival of the hot season caused Woolley and his colleagues to cease work. Throughout the summer they pondered over the problem until they finally came to the conclusion that it was, perhaps, not a floor at all, but rather the roof of some subterranean chamber—possibly the burial vault of a king. The more they thought about it, the more excited they became, and Woolley could hardly wait for the time to return to Ur.

When work was eventually resumed the surmise proved correct. The stones did represent the roof of a royal burial chamber; but, unfortunately, robbers had been there first and only a few fragments from a gold diadem and a group of badly corroded copper pots remained. Although this was bitterly disappointing, Woolley consoled himself with the thought that much valuable information had been gained concerning the ritual of burial in those remote times.

In the course of the season other chamber tombs were discovered; but these, too, had been broken into either by grave-diggers or by ancient treasure-hunters. In one area, however, there was some indication that the diggers were approaching an undisturbed grave. The workmen first encountered the mouth of a sloping trench in which were found the skeletons of five armed men. Although they were lying together in a group, they were accompanied by none of the normal grave-goods. When the bones had been photographed and carefully removed, the archaeologists found that the bodies had laid on a now much decayed matting carpet. With infinite care the sand and rubbish were brushed away to expose more of the carpet, which extended downwards, lying as it did on the inclining floor of the trench.

Before long the excavators came to more human remains, this time the skeletons of ten women laid out in two rows. The skulls were still adorned with elaborate golden head-dresses embellished with the pink of carnelian and the blue of lapis lazuli. Here again there were no funerary goods, none of cups, bowls, or personal possessions which the archaeologists had so frequently encountered in the individual graves. The only object accompanying the women was a single harp of magnificent workmanship, ornamented in gold, shell, and lapis. Although this relic was a discovery of the first order, it could hardly constitute the total funerary equipment of ten people.

Further investigation showed that the womens' bodies were not lying on the descending ramp, but were in the entrance to a large pit which was now to be excavated. Soon after this task was begun the first of a series of remarkable discoveries was made. This proved to be a sledge-like chariot mounted on runners instead of wheels and with woodwork decorated with golden lions' heads each with a mane of lapis lazuli, and with the heads of more lions and lionesses in silver. This magnificent vehicle had been drawn by two asses whose skeletal remains were lying in front of it. While the shaft to which their harnesses had been fastened had completely rotted away, the loop through which the reins had passed still survived. Fashioned in silver, it was surmounted by the golden figure of a donkey—one of the most delightful objects which have survived from the Sumerian civilization.

Lying near the chariot were a variety of weapons, tools, and domestic utensils along with an inlaid gaming-board of great beauty. Further careful excavating soon revealed more human skeletons and beyond them the remains of a large, mosaic-inlaid chest. The latter proved to be empty, but close by were found an astonishing quantity of vessels of gold, silver, copper, and stone. Woolley and his colleagues were naturally delighted with these finds; but they were still puzzled by one outstanding problem. Where was the person to whom all this magnificence belonged? Many skeletons had been found, but none gave any indication of being superior to the others.

The Queen's head-dress was an elaborate creation of gold ribbons and golden flowers, beech, and willow leaves.

Slowly and carefully all the objects were removed from the pit until, at last, only the shattered chest remained. When this, too, was moved the excavators discovered that it concealed a hole driven through a brick dome which clearly formed part of a burial chamber. Here, perhaps, they would find the owner of the treasure. But once again disappointment lay ahead, for the tomb proved to have been robbed and the chest had been placed so that it would conceal the damage to the roof.

While the final clearance was in progress in this area, the ramp leading to a second pit came into view. It was then that Woolley realized that he was dealing with two noble burials one above the other. The breached vault had nothing to do with the pit of the lion-headed chariot.

The latter, along with the diademed hand-maidens, belonged to another chamber tomb which was then still to be uncovered. When eventually this was reached, the archaeologists found that it had not been robbed and in it they discovered the body of Queen Shub-ad whose name appeared on a seal found in the entrance to the grave. She lay on a wooden bier, heavily adorned with jewellery. Her head-dress was an elaborate creation of gold ribbons and golden flowers, beech and willow leaves, the petals of the flowers ornamented with blue-and-white inlay. This garland was too large for the Queen's head and it is thought to have been fastened to an elaborate wig and held in place by a gold, five-toothed comb which was worn at the back of the head in the Spanish style. As if this creation were not enough, the Queen's ears were hung with gold rings which reached to her shoulders, while round her neck were necklaces which extended to her waist.

At the head and foot of the bier were found the skeletons of two female attendants, and scattered around them lay a mass of funerary offerings. There were bowls of gold, silver, copper, and stone as well as lamps and shells containing green cosmetics.

The queen's burial chamber had been dug down behind the tomb which had already been looted. It was therefore assumed that the latter belonged to Shub-ad's husband and that the looting had been carried out by grave-diggers immediately after her funeral and before the pit and ramp were sealed.

Digging below the level of the queen's ramp Woolley came to the entrance to the king's robbed tomb. Here he found the bones of six soldiers wearing copper helmets and carrying copper-headed spears. Behind them were the skeletons of six oxen which had drawn two wagons; but all that remained of the latter was a series of dirty marks in the ground. Nevertheless, careful excavating revealed that the wagons had solid wooden wheels and leather tyres.

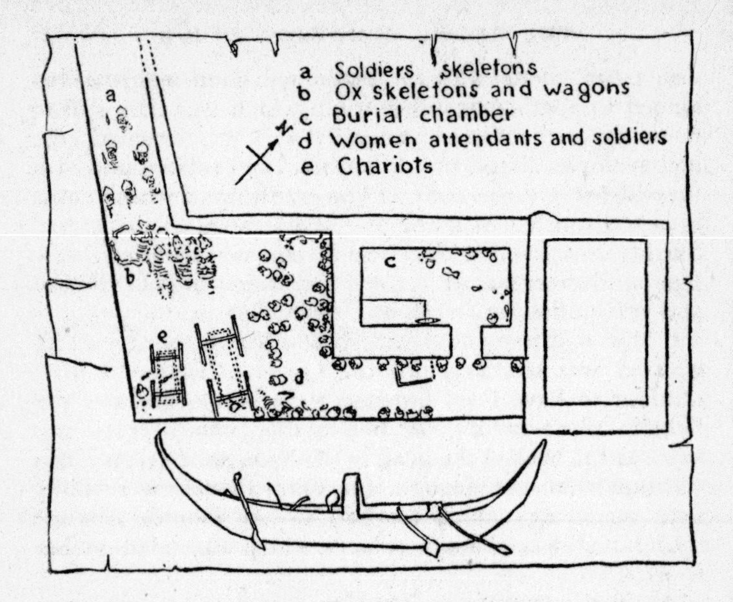


Plan of the entrance to a royal tomb. Below is a silver model of a boat found in the tomb—the same sort of rowing boat that can be seen on the Euphrates today.

(*From illustrations in* Ur of the Chaldees, *by Sir Leonard Woolley*)

Against one wall of the king's burial-chamber rested nine women atttendants, each wearing elaborate head-dresses and golden ear-rings. These women were lying on the ground with their heads pillowed against the wall of the tomb. Carefully laid on top of them were found two harps similar to the example found in the approach to the queen's tomb. As the excavation progressed it was found that the pit in front of the king's burial-chamber was crowded with human skeletons, some of them women, but many more of them soldiers still carrying their clusters of copper and gold-headed spears.

Fortunately the robbers' activities in the king's tomb had not been very thorough, with the result that a number of objects had been left behind. Among them were an inscribed seal naming the king as A-bar-gi and two model boats, one of copper and the other of silver. The first of the boats proved to be too badly corroded to be cleaned and restored, but the second turned out to be in a fine state of preservation. Sir Leonard Woolley later noted in his book, *Ur of the Chaldees*, that rowing-boats of almost identical design are still used amid the marshes of the Lower Euphrates not fifty miles from the site of Ur.

It is true that the finds from the royal cemetery at Ur were far less impressive than those which Howard Carter had found a few years previously in the tomb of Tutankhamen; but from an archaeological point of view the discoveries at Ur were much more important. Woolley's excavations had disclosed the funerary ritual of a civilization far older than that of the eighteenth dynasty Egyptian. His discoveries posed nearly as many questions as they answered. What, for example, was the belief of those people who seemed to have willingly gone to their death beside their late king and queen? What did they expect in the after-life, and into the hands of what god were their bodies commended?

Nowhere else in the civilized world was there a parallel to the funerary ritual of the kings and queens of Ur. Woolley was convinced that when a royal personage died, he or she was accompanied by all the members of their household. One pit alone contained the skeletal remains of six men and sixty-eight women, all in neat and tidy rows. Although it was never possible to determine exactly how these people died, there is every reason to believe that they entered the grave before death and ended their lives in peace and contentment. The delicate ornaments of the women were so neatly arranged that it seems impossible that they met a violent end. The most reasonable explanation may be that they were all heavily drugged before entering the grave. Later, an official went down into the pit among the sleeping women to make sure that they were in their right places and that their clothes and ornaments were looking their best. No other explanation would account for the harps which had been laid on top of the 'sleeping' gentlewomen.

During the excavations a considerable number of rich graves were found, many of them containing rare and beautiful treasures. But they were of little account when compared with the importance of Leonard Woolley's greatest archaeological discovery. Between the years 1927 and 1929 the clearance of the great cemetery had resulted in the digging of a giant pit some 200 feet long and between 30 and 40 feet in depth. At the bottom the excavators came to a thick bed of clay and it was this that proved to be the greatest discovery of all!

Digging below one of the royal tombs Woolley had found a group of inscribed tablets which dated the layer in which they were encountered to about the year 3000 B.C. A shaft dug below this stratum cut into the bed of water-deposited clay. When they reached it the experts at first believed that they had come to the bottom and that no more relics of human occupation would be found. Nevertheless the digging went on, and at a depth of a further 8 feet—to everyone's astonishment—the clay stopped and a new layer of domestic rubbish began. But the new finds were not in the least like objects from above the clay, for they were all of a much more primitive type. It seemed that the clay marked the end of one era and the beginning of another.

Ever since man first settled in the lower valleys of the Tigris and Euphrates his life and possessions have been endangered by the flooding of these rivers. Even today, in spite of modern engineering, the waters still threaten the land. Whenever the floods occur they leave behind them a deposit of silted clay; but it would require a flood of gigantic proportions to produce a layer 8 feet in depth. However, we do know of one flood which might have deposited this amount.

In the seventh chapter of the Book of Genesis we read that '. . . the same day were all the fountains of the great deep broken up, and the windows of heaven were opened. And the rain was upon the earth forty days and forty nights. . . . Fifteen cubits upward did the waters prevail; and the mountains were covered. . . . And the waters prevailed upon the earth a hundred and fifty days'. Only a flooding of the magnitude of this, the Biblical Deluge, could have produced so great a deposit of silt. Today it is generally agreed that Leonard Woolley had, in fact, discovered the residue of Noah's Flood, thus proving that the Bible story was not a myth but an historical fact. It was a classic example of something which occurs so often in archaeology—the excavator sets out to find one thing and ends up by discovering something entirely different. This, perhaps, is the secret of the romance of archaeology.

*CHAPTER THREE*

# THE TREASURES OF TUTANKHAMEN

THE discovery of the tomb of the young Pharaoh, Tutankhamen, undoubtedly created the greatest archaeological sensation that the world has yet seen. Nothing has so fired the popular imagination and no buried treasure has been so breathtaking as that which Howard Carter first located in November, 1922. Yet the contents of the tomb were no whit more astonishing than the extraordinary train of events which led up to the discovery, and the equally amazing story of greed, jealousy, and petty-mindedness which was to follow.

Not far from the town of Luxor in Upper Egypt lie the Theban Hills, and it was there, at the height of Egypt's imperial power, that the great kings of the eighteenth, nineteenth, and twentieth dynasties were laid to rest. Buried in fabulous splendour in tombs cut into the living rock, the Pharaohs hoped that their bodies would lie in peace for all time. But rarely did this happen. Within a few centuries and perhaps even within a generation after the tomb had been sealed, thieves would break in to rob the great man of his possessions.

Most of the Egyptian kings, from the first to the seventeenth dynasties (*c.* 3300 to 1580 B.C.), had been buried in ostentatious pomp beneath pyramid tombs guarded by custodians whose salaries were provided for in the wills of the dead rulers. These tombs, which were nothing short of Aladdins' caves, were naturally a constant challenge to any ambitious robber. Although the entrances were carefully sealed with blocks of stone weighing many tons, the thieves were often able to bribe the guards to help them in opening the tombs in exchange for a share of the loot. So successful were the robbers that by the beginning of the eighteenth dynasty (*c.* 1580 B.C.) there was hardly a single royal tomb in the whole of Egypt which had not been rifled.

Try as they might, the tomb-builders nearly always failed to outwit the thieves. Entrances were walled up, false tombs were built, secret doors fitted, and decoy passages and fake burial chambers were constructed in the hope of misleading the robbers; but all to no purpose. Eventually, the Pharaoh Thothmes I hit on the idea of keeping his burial place a secret. Instead of the magnificent funerals afforded to his predecessors he ordered that his body should be taken under cover of darkness and placed in a tomb hollowed out of the rock in a desolate, uninhabited valley in the Theban Hills. But even this strategy proved useless, for when the tomb was discovered in 1899 it contained nothing save an empty stone sarcophagus. Nevertheless, subsequent Pharaohs followed Thothmes I and insisted on being buried in secret tombs in the valley which has come to be known as the 'Valley of the Kings'.

As long ago as the year 1743 an English traveller named Richard Pococke visited the valley and described fourteen tombs which he had investigated. But at that time there were so many bandits lurking in the Theban Hills that no one dared stay long in the valley. It was not until 1815 that any serious digging was begun, at which time the work was supervised by a one-time circus strong man by the name of Belzoni. His efforts proved remarkably successful, although some of his methods were not exactly scientific. We may take as an example his use of a battering ram for opening sealed doorways. This is an instrument not normally carried by archaeologists.

Before leaving Egypt Belzoni stated that, in his opinion, the valley was exhausted and that no more tombs remained to be found. However, the display of treasures which he brought back, and which were exhibited at the Egyptian Hall in London, prompted many other expeditions to try their luck in the 'Valley of the Kings'.

In 1902 an American, Mr Theodore Davies, obtained permission from the Egyptian government to dig in the valley, and he continued to do so for twelve long years. At the end of that time he, too, decided that the valley was exhausted. In the meantime, Lord Carnarvon had been amusing himself excavating in and around the ancient city of Thebes, and when the American ceased working in the valley, Carnarvon applied for a concession to continue there. The concession was granted and, assisted by his more experienced friend Howard Carter, he started to dig.

Howard Carter was the son of an animal painter and was, himself, a gifted draughtsman. It was in this capacity that he first went to Egypt to work for Professor Percy Newberry who was then excavating the remains of an important temple. Later, Carter left Professor Newberry to become Chief Inspector of Antiquities for Upper Egypt. Those who knew him described Carter as a man who had the ability to get the best out of his Egyptian workmen, but who was quick-tempered and often quarrelled with the authorities with whom he had to work. This last facet of his character was to play an important part in the events which were to follow.

When Carter and Lord Carnarvon began to work in the valley, they decided to go over the entire area systematically. To do this they made out a map of the ground and divided it up into squares, each of which was to be carefully explored before being ticked off on the plan. Off and on for ten years Carter laboured in the valley and at the end of that time he had very little to show for his efforts. By then the first World War was over and money was becoming increasingly difficult to find. In the summer of 1922 Lord Carnarvon invited Carter to visit him at his home at Highclere Castle. On arrival Carter was told that the results of the excavations had not justified the cost and, regretfully, Lord Carnarvon would put up no more money. Work would, therefore, have to be abandoned at once.

Carter pleaded to be allowed to continue for one more season. He was convinced, he said, that another tomb still remained to be found. Only one area of their map was yet to be investigated and this was piled high with a mountain of soil and stones which had been excavated from the nearby tomb of Rameses VI. Reluctantly, Lord Carnarvon agreed that this section should be explored before they gave up. Carter accordingly returned to Egypt at the end of October, 1922, and by the beginning of November he was ready to start work.

On the 4 November, Carter's workmen discovered the top of a stairway leading downwards, and throughout the following day they laboured feverishly to clear away the debris which covered it. As each step was revealed the excitement mounted until, just before sunset, the top of a doorway began to appear. The entrance was found to be blocked and covered with plaster which bore the impressions of seals. As Carter peered at these stamps in the failing light in the hope that they would give some clue as to who might lie inside, he noticed that at one point some of the plaster had fallen away. Eagerly he made a small hole large enough to take an electric torch. As he peered into the hole the light revealed a passage blocked with rubble from floor to ceiling, indicating, apparently, that no robber had passed that way since the entrance was filled.

Carter was overjoyed. 'Alone, save for my native workmen,' he wrote, 'I found myself, after years of comparatively unproductive labour, on the threshold of what might prove to be a magnificent discovery. Anything, literally anything, might lie beyond that passage, and it needed all my self-control to keep from breaking down the doorway, and investigating then and there.'

Instead, Carter filled in the hole, set guards over the

excavation and sent a cable to Lord Carnarvon who was still in England. 'At last have made wonderful discovery in valley,' he wired, 'a magnificent tomb with seals intact; re-covering same for your arrival; congratulations.'

Towards the end of November Lord Carnarvon and his daughter arrived, and the entrance was once again cleared, this time in its entirety. When this task was completed two features were revealed; firstly, that the seal impressions in the plaster were those of the young king Tutankhamen, and secondly that part of the doorway had been replastered at a later date, indicating that robbers had, after all, entered the tomb. When all the filling in front of the doorway had been removed it became evident that the thieves had tunnelled through the rubble filling of the passage and that when the robbery was discovered their route had been plugged with more rubble.

It took a whole day to remove the debris from the passage, but when it was completed another sealed doorway was revealed. Trembling with excitement, Carter made a small hole in the upper left-hand corner. A candle held aloft flickered furiously as a draught of musty air rushed out. There was a long pause while Carter's eyes adjusted themselves to the wavering light. Meanwhile, Carnarvon, his daughter, and their assistants waited impatiently and with bated breath for Carter's report. This was the greatest moment of his life and it is only fitting that Carter, himself, should describe what he saw.

'. . . as my eyes grew accustomed to the light, details of the room within emerged slowly from the mist, strange animals, statues, and gold—everywhere the glint of gold. For the moment—an eternity it must have seemed to the others standing by—I was struck dumb with amazement, and when Lord Carnarvon, unable to stand the suspense any longer, inquired anxiously, "Can you see anything?" it was all I could do to get out the words, "Yes, wonderful things".'

The first things to catch the eye were three great gilt couches, their sides in the shape of thin, long-legged animals. All around the chamber were painted and inlaid caskets, chairs, stools, beds, a golden throne, and a confused pile of dismantled, gilded chariots, their wheels stacked against the wall. At the far end of the room, facing each other, stood two life-size statues of a king painted black, wearing gold kilts, gilded sandals, and draped in the remains of linen shawls. The scene was magnificent beyond all dreams. But one important feature was missing—the sarcophagus of the king!

Disappointment turned to yet greater excitement when the excavators realized that they were not looking into a burial chamber, but only into an ante-room. At the far end, between the black sentinels, Carter could see that the wall was not solid like the other three, but was merely plastered and sealed as was the entrance through which he was peering.

'We were but on the threshold of our discovery', he wrote. 'Beyond the guarded door there was to be another chamber, possibly a succession of them, and in one of them beyond any shadow of doubt, in all his magnificent panoply of death, we should find the Pharaoh lying.'

'We had seen enough, and our brains began to reel at the thought of the task in front of us. We re-closed the hole, locked the wooden grille which had been placed upon the first doorway, left our native staff on guard, mounted our donkeys, and rode home down the Valley, strangely silent and subdued.'

When the ante-chamber was eventually opened a careful examination of the blocked doorway beyond showed that this, too, had been breached by the thieves, only to be carefully resealed by the ancient officials. The seals stamped over the undisturbed areas of plaster were all those of Tutankhamen, and there was now little doubt that his body would be discovered in one of the inner chambers.

Further traces of the tomb-robbers were revealed when

Carter peered under one of the couches—there in the wall was a hole just large enough for a small man to crawl through.

Carter chanced to bend down and peer under one of the couches, for there, at floor level, was a hole in the wall just large enough for a small man to crawl through. Shining a torch into the opening Carter could see into another chamber which was littered with overturned boxes, alabaster vases, baskets and furniture. The room had clearly been ransacked by the thieves, who were searching for small but valuable objects which could easily be carried away. Yet more evidence of their activity was later found in the ante-room, where a number of gold finger-rings were discovered tied up in a scarf.

The presence of the wrapped rings indicated that the thieves had either been caught or had abandoned their work in some haste. If, in fact, the robbers were caught, we must assume one of two things, either that they were actually apprehended in the tomb or that they were seized soon after leaving, in which case the rings and other portable objects must have been brought back by the authorities who were responsible for having tidied up the ante-chamber. There was evidence that this had been done, for many of the trinkets and statues had been heaped into the wrong boxes, while the furniture had been piled unceremoniously against the walls.

No effort had been made to tidy the second room, the annexe, nor to close up the hole in its wall. Hastily, the officials had retraced their steps, resealing the ante-chamber, reblocking the passage, and then sealing up the outer doorway. One can imagine their relief when they escaped from this house of the dead into the bright Egyptian sunlight. Finally the entrance was filled in and a load of soil and stones spread over the top to hide it. Thus it remained for three thousand years.

Earlier archaeological excavations had more than once come within an ace of finding the entrance; but for one reason or another fate had preserved it. Carter himself had dug twice within two yards of the steps, once during the early days of his partnership with Lord Carnarvon and once previously when working with Theodore Davies, the American. On that occasion the tomb had been missed because, at the last minute, Davies had decided to shift his workmen to a more promising site!

When Carter realized that another chamber lay beyond the statue-guarded doorway, it was as much as he could do to refrain from breaking in there and then. But he knew that by doing so he would almost certainly damage some of the priceless objects which littered the ante-chamber. These things would, therefore, have to be carefully removed beforehand.

To the layman, this task might seem fairly simple; no more difficult than moving house. In point of fact, Carter and Lord Carnarvon were faced with one of the most delicate and hazardous undertakings that have ever fallen to an archaeologist. While some of the finds were in an astonishingly good state of preservation, others threatened to fall to pieces at a touch. Sandals composed of countless beads appeared perfectly preserved, but had they been picked up, the handler would have found them to be no more than a heap of beads which would have rolled away like 'hundreds and thousands' across the floor of the chamber. These and many other fragile objects had to be encased in paraffin wax before they could be moved. The funerary bouquets, for example, could only be handled after being sprayed with two or three coats of a cellulose solution. The work was slow and often frustrating.

Luckily, it was possible to commandeer two nearby tombs which were now empty and could be turned into a photographic darkroom and a laboratory where the less fragile relics could be taken for treatment. The remainder had to be temporarily treated and reinforced on the spot. It would have been so easy to have hurried through these tasks, carefully treating only the finest objects and trusting to luck with the rest. But Carter would not hear of it.

Describing the duties of an archaeologist to his discoveries Carter wrote: 'The things he finds are not his own property, to treat as he pleases, or neglect as he chooses. They are a direct legacy from the past to the present age . . . and if, by carelessness, slackness, or ignorance, he lessens the sum of knowledge that might have been obtained from them, he knows himself to be guilty of an archaeological crime of the first magnitude. Destruction of evidence is so painfully easy, and yet so hopelessly irreparable.' Those words, written in 1923, when the tomb was still being cleared, are as true today as they were then. They could well be memorized as a creed by every aspiring archaeologist.

The difficulty of removing the hundreds of objects from the ante-chamber was not the greatest of Carter's worries. Ever since the first news of the discovery leaked out, the press of the world had gathered in the valley, recording every word and movement that he made. The name of Tutankhamen was heard in every continent, and hordes of sightseers poured into the Theban Hills intent on seeing the tomb. Letters reached Carter from the far corners of the earth, many of them from cranks and more from people who wanted to be personally shown round. Egyptian government officials sent their friends and relations to see inside the ante-chamber and for diplomatic reasons they could not be refused. Nevertheless, every visitor who entered the tomb delayed the work until he or she had departed. By the time a dozen or more V.I.P.'s had been escorted through and the details pointed out to them a whole day was wasted.

Much more worrying was the constant fear that visitors would unintentionally damage some of the fragile objects which were heaped in such profusion in the chamber. One had only to take a single hasty step to bring the piled furniture and boxes crashing to the floor. Fellow experts were naturally welcomed, for they needed no urging to take care and, besides, their comments and suggestions were often of assistance. But the casual visitor, on the other hand, could only be a danger and a time-waster. Many of these people came, armed with letters of introduction, not because they were in the least interested in archaeology, but because the fact of having seen inside the tomb marked them as privileged persons.

'Can you imagine anything more maddening,' complained Carter, 'when you are completely absorbed in some difficult problem, than to give up half an hour of your precious time to a visitor who has pulled every conceivable wire to gain admittance, and then to hear him say quite audibly as he goes away, "Well, there wasn't much to see, after all"? This actually happened last winter—and more than once.'

Working under those conditions it was hardly surprising that tempers wore a little thin. Many people were turned away and so went back angrily to Luxor and Cairo complaining of Carter's ill-manners, selfishness, boorishness, and anything else that they could think up. To make matters worse, similar opinions were being aired in the columns of the world's press.

So many newspaper men had besieged the tomb when first it was discovered that Lord Carnarvon had decided to put a stop to the constant wrangling for news by giving the exclusive rights in both pictures and information to *The Times*. But instead of providing a happy solution to the problem, this move created a surge of ill-feeling among the assembled reporters. While *The Times*' representative was free to go in and out of the tomb, keeping up to date with every development, the rest of the world's press was forced to make do with rumours, scandal, and second-hand information picked up in hotel bars in Cairo. It is not surprising, therefore, that many of the published stories turned out to be inaccurate, highly coloured, and harshly critical of Carter and his colleagues.

The scene in the valley resembled a desert Derby Day. The approach road was jammed with vehicles and every kind of animal which could be induced to carry a tourist, while at the entrance to the tomb unofficial guides, sellers of antiquities (most of them fakes), and the hawkers of soft drinks were all doing a roaring trade. Under the circumstances, it is hardly to be wondered at that the excavators' one wish was for the whole lot to go away and leave them in peace.

However, regardless of constant interruptions, the work of clearing the ante-chamber went on until, by the middle of February, 1923, only the two sentinel statues remained. On the 17th of that month Carter was ready to open the sealed doorway. Twenty chairs were arranged in the ante-chamber for the benefit of the select few who were invited to witness the opening. Among the privileged were Carter's fellow archaeologists, government and museum officials, *The Times*' correspondent, and other distinguished guests. Shortly after 2 p.m. Carter and Lord Carnarvon began to remove the sealing plaster. After ten

# TUTANKHAMEN'S TOMB

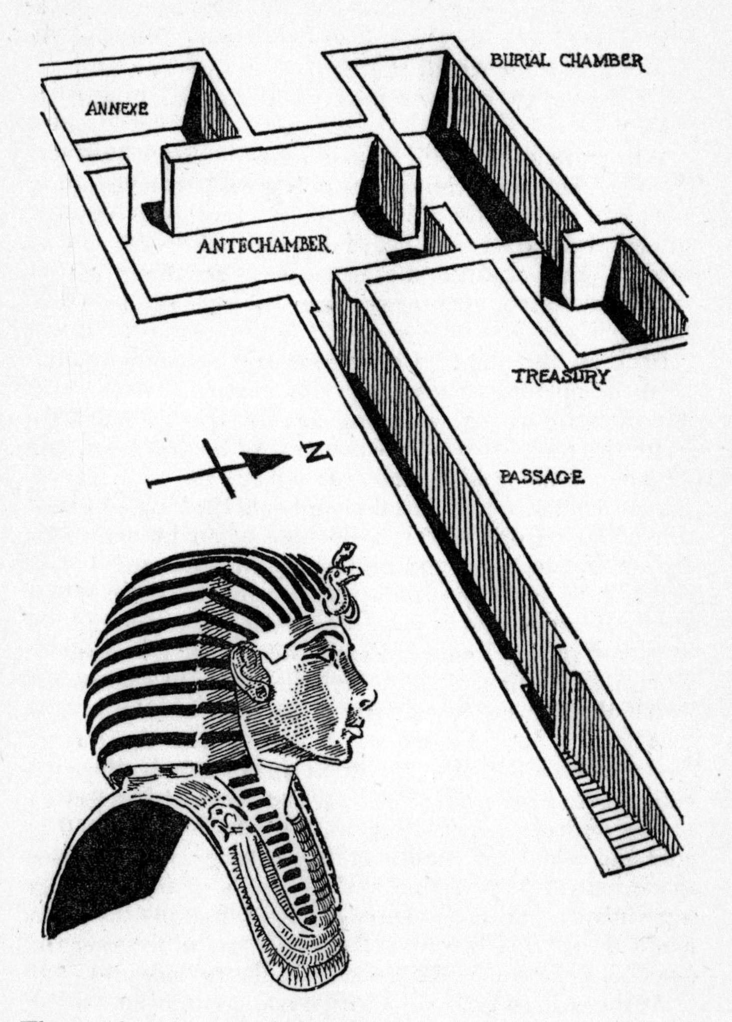


The tomb was entered through the ante-chamber. One by one the stones had to be removed from the wall.

minutes of silent chipping the hole was large enough for a torch to be inserted. No one really knew what to expect, but nevertheless they were totally unprepared for the astonishing sight which the light revealed. The rays fell abruptly on to what seemed to be a solid wall of gold.

With infinite care the stones were removed from the doorway, and every minute the hole grew larger, revealing more and more of the golden wall. The buzz of excitement among the guests was heard by the hundreds waiting outside, and at once the news of a startling, but as yet unidentified, discovery was racing through the valley.

Back in the tomb, Carter was still removing stones from the opening, fearing every moment that one would slip inwards and go crashing against the golden wall. 'With the removal of a very few stones,' he said later, 'the mystery of the golden wall was solved. We were at the entrance of the actual burial-chamber of the king, and that which barred our way was the side of an immense gilt shrine built to cover and protect the sarcophagus. It was visible now from the ante-chamber by the light of the standard lamps, and as stone after stone was removed, and its gilded surface came gradually into view, we could, as though by electric current, feel the tingle of excitement which thrilled the spectators.'

When, at last, Carter was able to enter the burial-chamber he found that the great shrine almost filled the entire room from walls to ceiling, and measured 17 feet by 11 feet and was 9 feet in height, the sides being coated in gold and inlaid with panels of blue faience. In the narrow space between the shrine and the walls of the chamber were heaped various funerary emblems, notably the seven magical oars which were intended for use in ferrying the dead king across the dark waters of the underworld.

At the eastern end of the shrine two great folding doors were found bolted but not sealed. Had the thieves reached the body of the king? With pounding heart Carter drew back the bolts and swung the doors open to reveal the *sealed* doors of another gilded shrine. The king was safe.

To have broken the seals and opened the second shrine might well have caused damage to the first. As Carter explained afterwards, a feeling of intrusion had descended on him and he lost any desire to penetrate further. Carefully and reverently he closed the outer doors and left the king to sleep a little longer in peace.

An examination of the burial chamber itself revealed an unsealed doorway at its northern end leading into yet another room, which proved to contain the greater part of the treasure. Here were rows of chests and black cabinet shrines, all save one of which were securely sealed. The single box whose doors stood open contained statues of Tutankhamen standing on black leopards. Just inside the doorway of the room crouched a figure of Anubis, the jackal god, resting on a massive ceremonial sledge. Behind it lay the gilded, life-size head of a bull, while distributed round the chamber were a number of model boats, some fully rigged. The room also contained the now familiar array of furniture and dismantled chariots. At the northern end stood a great, gilded, wooden canopy under which rested a massive shrine-like chest. Carter realized at once that this would contain the four canopic jars which held those parts of the king's intestines which had been removed by the embalmers.

A week after the opening of the burial-chamber the tomb was locked and the entrance filled in, for the winter was over and the hot season was already beginning. It was therefore thought prudent to remove no more objects for fear that the extreme changes of temperature might damage them.

During the weeks which immediately preceded the opening of the burial-chamber the popular press made repeated attacks on Lord Carnarvon, accusing him of exploiting the tomb for his own ends, creating a news monopoly, and of behaving as though he were digging up the graves of his own ancestors in the Welsh mountains. These and many other unpleasant gibes caused Carnarvon both worry and distress, and it was obvious to everyone associated with him that he was approaching a state of nervous exhaustion. In March he quarrelled with Carter, claiming that part of the treasure should be his property. His friend violently disagreed. Harsh words were exchanged and the two parted, vowing never to work together again. Soon after this unhappy quarrel a mosquito bite turned septic, pneumonia developed, and on the 6th of April Lord Carnarvon died.

The press, ever eager for a sensation, suggested that he had died as a result of an ancient curse laid on anyone who disturbed the tomb of Tutankhamen. This piece of groundless journalism has since grown into a healthy legend. Indeed, it has blossomed to such a degree that many people believe that all the excavators were struck down within a few years of entering the tomb. Nothing could be further from the truth.

In the autumn of 1924 Carter returned to Egypt to continue where he and his friend had left off. The tomb was reopened and work immediately began on the difficult task of dismantling the golden shrines. There were, in fact, four of them, one inside the other like a nest of Chinese boxes, each one more magnificent than the last. Finally Carter reached the great, quartzite sarcophagus, which was found to be adorned with four guardian goddesses, one carved in high relief at each corner. The lid was of granite, but had been tinted to match the yellow of the sarcophagus.

Before another invited audience, the lid, which weighed more than a ton, was slowly raised on block and tackle to reveal a linen-shrouded human shape. One after another the shrouds were drawn aside until, with a gasp from the assembled audience, the last fell away. There, filling the whole of the inside of the sarcophagus, lay a magnificent gilded coffin in human shape and inlaid with coloured glass which blazed like jewels in the glare of the lights. The

There lay a magnificent gilded coffin in human shape.

head was clearly a portrait of the young Tutankhamen, and the hands were crossed over the chest holding the Crook and Flail, the emblems of sovereignty.

A week later, just when the newspaper-reading public was agog with excitement, Carter created his greatest sensation by announcing that having been made subject to so many restrictions and interferences by government departments, he proposed to close the tomb and cease work indefinitely. This was the climax to months of friction between the excavators and the Egyptian Service of Antiquities. Much of the trouble had been caused by the fact that the estate of Lord Carnarvon was claiming part of the treasure on behalf of his widow, and on Carter's side by his objection to the government's constant meddling with the way in which the excavation was being conducted.

The outcome was simply that the Egyptians cancelled Lady Carnarvon's permit to work in the valley and forbade Carter to enter the tomb. Just to show who was master, the Egyptian authorities immediately opened the tomb to the public—providing a firework display to mark the occasion.

Carter retaliated by suing the Egyptian government on behalf of the Carnarvon estate. At the subsequent court hearing more bitter words were uttered and Carter's counsel even went so far as to accuse the Egyptian government of breaking into the tomb like a bandit. Uproar in court! As a result of these ill-chosen words the Egyptians were even more firmly resolved to keep the British out of the tomb. Carter departed on a world lecture tour heartbroken and embittered.

In November 1924, the head of the Egyptian army was assassinated, enabling Britain to take a much firmer grip on Egyptian affairs. Consequently, Carter was told that he could continue his work in the tomb. He was eventually ready to start at the end of January 1925. But by then little time remained before the summer sun would again be blazing down into the valley. Nevertheless, Carter decided to complete the clearance of the burial chamber before any further complications could arise.

Once again the shrouds were removed from the gilded coffin and so, too, was the little garland of flowers which rested on the brow—put there, perhaps, by the mourning hands of the young, widowed queen. Then the lid of the coffin was raised on pulleys to expose another shrouded figure, on which lay garlands of lotus petals, cornflowers, and olive and willow leaves. The shroud concealed a second gilded coffin more striking than the first. This coffin could not be opened without being lifted bodily from the outer case, and those who handled it were astonished at its weight, eight strong men being needed to move it.

Eventually the lid of the second coffin was raised to reveal yet another decaying shroud through which the now familiar glint of gold could be seen. It was not until this, the third coffin, was lifted that the astonishing weight was explained. Here was no wooden coffin coated with gold leaf and set with coloured glass; this was of solid gold inlaid with semi-precious stones!

When the gold coffin was finally opened, Carter and his friends were at last in the presence of the dead king. There lay the mummy, carefully swathed in its linen wrappings and with a portrait mask of beaten gold fitting closely over the head and shoulders. Unhappily, the mummy proved to be in very poor shape. The resinous unguents and libations which had been poured over the body before the coffin was closed had caused the wrappings to become carbonized, making them as brittle as charred paper, while the entire mummy was found to have stuck to the bottom of the coffin.

It was not until the wrappings were removed that the assembled experts realized just how faithfully the ancient artists and goldsmiths had portrayed their 18-year-old king. The arms were heavily hung with bracelets and the fingers adorned with rings of the finest workmanship, while over the body itself lay innumerable golden charms and ornaments. The feet rested on golden sandals and each toe was enclosed within a thimble-shaped case of gold. Piece by piece the treasures were removed until eventually only the frail body remained.

The examination of the mummy completed the 1925 season's work; but there was still much to be done. Neither the annexe nor the inner treasure chamber had been touched, and both would have to wait until the following autumn. In all, the total clearance of the tomb took ten seasons of hard, nerve-racking work which continued long after the world had lost interest in Tutankhamen and his tomb amid the Theban Hills.

Today, the treasures are displayed, restored to all their original splendour, in the galleries of the Cairo Museum. When all was over, it was tactfully suggested to the Egyptian government that it might be a generous way of rewarding Carter and his little band of British and American colleagues, to present a selection of the duplicated objects from the tomb to the British Museum and to the Metropolitan Museum of Art in New York. But not one stick, stone, or grain of sand did they receive.

*CHAPTER FOUR*

# THE BOY WHO DREAMED OF TROY

This is the story of a boy who believed in fairy tales and who, when he grew up, proved to the world that even the most fanciful stories may often contain a germ of truth. The boy was Heinrich Schliemann, the son of an impoverished Protestant pastor at the village of Ankershagen in the North German duchy of Mecklenburg-Schwerin. Little Heinrich, who was only one year old when he arrived in the village, was destined to remain there for eight more—years which were to be among the most important in all his long life.

Like so many German villages, Ankershagen was well stocked with tales of ogres, werewolves, and all the other midnight creatures which flit across the moonlit pages of Teutonic folklore. Far from being afraid of these stories, Heinrich revelled in them, believing every gruesome word, yet always asking for more. His summer-house was said to be haunted by the ghost of his father's predecessor, while a pond close to the garden was believed to be occupied by a ghostly maiden who rose up from the dark waters every midnight clutching a silver bowl. A burial mound close by was claimed to house the child of a long-dead robber chieftain who had laid it to rest in a golden cradle. But these were secondary legends when compared with the tale of the black-hearted Henning von Holstein, once owner of the local mediaeval castle.

The story told how one of Henning's evil plans had been thwarted by a cowherd from the village, and how the villain seized the unfortunate servant and roasted him alive in a giant frying-pan, finally kicking the poor creature with his left foot. Eventually, when retribution overtook him, Henning buried his treasure close to the castle and tried to escape. But he was soon caught, and to avoid justice he committed suicide. A long line of stones in the grave-yard were said to mark his resting-place, and the legend had it that every year Henning's left leg, garbed in a black stocking, grew out of the ground beside the stones.

The young Heinrich was fascinated by this gruesome story and frequently visited the graveyard in the hope of seeing Henning's stockinged leg. When it failed to appear he would go to his father and beg him to excavate the body of Henning to see what had gone wrong. His request having been refused, the boy would reassure himself of the truth of the story by inspecting a walled-up fireplace in the ruined castle which was supposed to be the place where the luckless cowherd had fried. Heinrich remembered that the legend told how Henning had tried to hide the scene of his crime by bricking up the fireplace, and how the fates had decreed that it would always remain visible so that the ghastly deed would never be forgotten. Sure enough the new brickwork could clearly be distinguished from the old, and the boy accepted the whole story without question—just as in later life he was to accept other legends with equal readiness.

The boy's father would often talk to him of the wonders of the ancient world, although he, the pastor, knew comparatively little about it. Nevertheless the young Heinrich listened eagerly, and when at Christmas, 1829, he was given a history book containing a fanciful engraving of the legendary city of Troy his gratitude knew no bounds. But he was a little incredulous when his father explained that the city with its great walls had vanished from the face of the earth. He would argue for hours, claiming that the foundations of Troy must still be there, though buried beneath the dust of time. Firmly, he announced that when he grew up he would find the site and dig up the city just to prove his point.

At the age of fourteen, still dreaming of Troy and the heroes of the Trojan War, Heinrich had to give up his schooling to become apprenticed to a grocer, a position which he retained for five and a half years. At the end of that time the young man strained himself while lifting a cask, and so was unable to be of any further use to the grocer. After going to Hamburg and losing two jobs through his inability to lift heavy weights, Heinrich Schliemann went to sea as a cabin-boy aboard the brig *Dorothea.* But fate decreed that his marine career would be short, for two weeks after signing on, the ship was wrecked in a storm off the Dutch island of Texel. While no lives were lost, the *Dorothea* was a total wreck and the crew were deprived of all their possessions—all that is, save Schliemann, whose box was washed ashore next day. This stroke of luck was to mark a turning point in the young man's fortunes.

After obtaining a job in Holland which enabled him to feed himself, Schliemann set out to improve his education, first by teaching himself penmanship and then by learning English. To improve his memory he contrived to memorize the whole of *The Vicar of Wakefield* as well as Sir Walter Scott's *Ivanhoe,* exercises which enabled him to teach himself French, Dutch, Spanish, Portuguese, and Russian! His diligence earned him a post in a merchant's office and then a position as his firm's representative in St Petersburg. Later, he opened his own business in that city and soon built himself up into an international concern, making a deal of money out of other people's misfortunes during the Crimean War. Eventually, at the age of 46, Schliemann, now a man of immense wealth, was able to turn his mind to the dreams of his childhood.

With his Greek wife, Sophia, Schliemann crossed the Hellespont and arrived on the plain of Troy bearing a copy of Homer's *Iliad* before him like a banner. The noble tales which he knew by heart—and believed in just as firmly as he had the legend of Henning von Holstein—would provide him with all the information he needed. All he had to do—so he thought—was to follow the *Iliad* to the letter and he would find the lost city of Troy. Many scholars who had heard of his quest openly scorned him as a wealthy eccentric. How, they argued, could any thinking man believe these fairy tales? Did they not tell of gods turning into mortals to aid the cause of right? Only a lunatic would take such legends seriously. But Schliemann was undaunted.

It would be wrong to assume that Schliemann was the first to champion the existence of Troy. A number of scholars had made similar claims before him, asserting that the city must have been situated a three-hour journey from the coast near a village named Bounarbashi. Therefore, *Iliad* in hand, Schliemann made straight for this spot and proceeded to consider whether it fitted the scene as described by Homer. The supporters of the site had recalled that the ancient writer had mentioned two springs, one hot and one cold, and they had pointed out that two such springs still flowed below the village. Schliemann duly examined the site and sure enough there were two springs—but there were also thirty-eight others—all of them cold. He remembered that the *Iliad* stated that Hector and Achilles ran three times round the city, and so to test the prevailing theory Schliemann himself set out to run three times round the hill on which stood Bounarbashi. He soon discovered that the only possible route which the heroes could have taken led away to the south.

'I went myself down by this side,' wrote Schliemann, 'which falls off at first at an angle of 45°, and afterwards at an angle of about 25°; thus, I was forced to crawl backwards on all fours: it took me a quarter of an hour to come down, and I carried away the conviction that no mortal being, not even a goat, has ever been able to run swiftly down a slope which descends at an angle of 25°; and that Homer never intended to make us believe that

Hector and Achilles, in making the circuit of the city, could have run down this impossible descent.'

These were not the only objections to Bounarbashi as the site of Homeric Troy. There was also the problem of its distance from the shores where the Greek ships had moored. Using Homer as literally as one would contemporary battle despatches, Schliemann deduced that Troy could not possibly have stood more than three miles inland from the sea. The distance from Bounarbashi measured nine miles to the coast. Any further doubt left Schliemann's mind when he found that the hill had yielded little pottery and no sign of building materials. He was convinced that this was not the site of Troy.

Only three miles from the seas stood another hill, and this too had been claimed as the site of the ancient city. Here the evidence seemed stronger, for not only had pottery and foundations been unearthed, but as long ago as the first century A.D. the Greek geographer Strabo had described the hill as 'the new Ilium'. Before long Schliemann had made up his mind that this hill, now known as Hissarlik, had once been the site of ancient Troy. He later quoted in evidence an extremely thin argument put forward by a certain Major Rennell which goes more or less as follows. Knowing that Alexander the Great had once been shown the site of Troy, and that Alexander was both scholar and military tactician, the major reasoned that he would have known whether he was being shown the correct site. Had Alexander been taken to Bounarbashi he would surely have rejected it. As the great man did not do so, it followed, apparently automatically, that he had been brought to Hissarlik. This was therefore the site of Homeric Troy.

Even if Schliemann could be accused of building his deductions on the weakest of foundations, there can be no denying that he was endowed with astonishing luck—an attribute that even the most brilliant modern archaeologist needs if he is to succeed. In 1870, he began to dig at Hissarlik, and he soon discovered that he was dealing with a vast accumulation of ancient refuse which had grown up on a long-inhabited site. The complexity could be compared with that which Sir Leonard Woolley was later to find at Ur of the Chaldees. At a depth of 16 feet Schliemann came upon a massive stone wall, 6½ feet in thickness, which he decided was part of a tower dating from the Macedonian era. This first season's digging constituted no more than an exploratory sortie to enable Schliemann to gain some idea of the problems which faced him.

In 1871 the German returned to Hissarlik to commence a full season's intensive excavating. With him came his wife, whose beauty had been likened to that of the incomparable Helen of Troy. Writing of his wife's arrival, Schliemann described her as '. . . a native of Athens and a warm admirer of Homer, and who, with glad enthusiasm, joined me in executing the great work which, nearly half a century ago, my childish simplicity had agreed upon with my father.'

In the autumn of 1871, supported by more than eighty unskilled labourers and equipped only with 'pickaxes, wooden shovels, baskets, and eight wheelbarrows', Schliemann proceeded to dig a trench through the northern slope of the hill to a depth of 33 feet. Down he went, tearing aside the foundations of numerous structures which he encountered on the way, but salvaging vast quantities of pottery and other small objects. After a pause during the winter, work began again in March 1872, this time with a hundred and thirty men armed 'with the best English wheelbarrows, pickaxes, and spades'. At a depth of 53 feet the diggers finally reached bed-rock. This achieved, Schliemann turned his attention to the south side of the hill and proceeded to drive another gigantic trench into it. Almost nonchalantly he cut through layer after layer, tossing aside anything and everything which seemed to have no bearing on his main objective.

The story of the Wooden Horse of Troy had excited Heinrich as a boy. He was determined to find the Lost City.

'As it was my object to excavate Troy,' wrote Schliemann, 'which I expected to find in one of the lower cities, I was forced to demolish many interesting ruins in the upper strata; as, for example, at a depth of 20 feet below the surface, the ruins of a prehistoric building 10 feet high. . . . The building evidently belonged to the fourth of the enormous strata of debris in succession from the virgin soil; and if, as cannot be doubted, each stratum represents the ruins of a distinct city, it belongs to the fourth city.'

Even in the course of modern scientific excavating it is often necessary to record and then destroy later material in pursuit of earlier deposits. But the irony of Schliemann's story lay in the fact that he was unable to recognize Homeric Troy when he found it. There were nine cities in all, one on top of the other, and of these, the second and third from the bottom possessed huge foundations and showed clear evidence of having suffered through fire. Schliemann decided that one of the latter must represent the Troy of the wooden horse. But the sad truth was that this city was represented not by the second or third layers but by the sixth—much of which had been destroyed en route to the earlier levels.

As the year 1872 progressed, work went furiously on, turning the once serene hill of Hissarlik into something resembling an open-cast mining project. In his account of the work Schliemann again states with pride how he had supplied his army of workmen with '10 hand-carts and 88 wheelbarrows to work with, in addition to which I kept 6 horse-carts . . . Besides screw-jacks, chains, and windlasses, implements consisted of 24 large iron levers, 108 spades, and 103 pickaxes, all of the best English manufacture.'

In the February of the following year Schliemann and his wife were again hard at work. Having previously built himself a house on the site, they found themselves forced to abandon it to the senior workmen, who had insufficient clothing to keep them warm through the bitter Turkish winter. They therefore took over one of the draughty wooden huts, feeling themselves better equipped to endure the cold.

'My poor wife and myself, therefore, suffered very much, since the icy north wind, which recals [*sic*] Homer's frequent mention of the blasts of Boreas, blew with such violence through the chinks of our house-walls, which were made of planks, that we were not even able to light our lamps in the evening; and although we had fire on the hearth, yet the thermometer showed 23 Fahrenheit, while the water which stood near the hearth froze into solid masses. During the day we could to some degree bear the cold by working in the excavations, but in the evenings we had nothing to keep us warm except our enthusiasm for the great work of discovering Troy.'

Whatever people may say today of Schliemann's excavating methods, no one can deny that here was a man dedicated beyond all reason to the goal on which he had set his heart. He was a millionaire, able to sleep and idle away his declining years, wanting nothing that money could buy. Yet here he was, trying to keep warm in a draught-ridden wooden shack, having given up his newly-built house to provide comfort for his precious workmen. Schliemann knew that if his men became ill, the work would slow down and perhaps come to a complete halt, and he would rather die of cold than live to see this happen.

As the weather improved, the tempo of work increased, and Schliemann, in his account of the operations, described his methods of digging in a hurry. 'In this new trench I had first to break through a wall 10 feet thick, consisting of large blocks of marble . . . then I had to pierce the wall of Lysimachus, which was also 10 feet thick, and built of large hewn stones. Besides this we had to cut our way through two Trojan walls. . . .'

After describing the uncovering of the supposed temple of Athene which belonged to the later Ilium, Schliemann went on to state that, 'In order to bring Troy itself to light, I was forced to sacrifice the ruins of this temple, of which I left standing only some parts of the north and south walls.' The German seems to have felt no guilt, and he wrote these passages as simple statements of fact, and not as the confessions which they should surely be.

At the very end of the 1873 season Schliemann was to make a discovery which was as yet unparalleled in the annals of archaeology. Once again it was his phenomenal luck which saved the day, for had he not been on the right spot at the right moment, the 'Treasure of Priam' might have been lost into the pockets of the none too honest workmen. With the season nearly over, no one expected that anything more would be found—no one, that is, except Schliemann himself, who still behaved as though it were just beginning. His eyes firmly riveted on the

He noticed a copper object protruding from the loosened soil, and behind it was a glint of gold.

ground, he watched his workmen as they dug, trying to ensure that not one stone or sherd should pass unnoticed.

While inspecting a piece of masonry at a depth of 28 feet, he noticed a copper object protruding from the loosened soil, and behind it he recognized the glint of gold. A modern archaeologist's first task would have been carefully to expose the objects with brush, trowel, and spoon, ensuring that every object should be drawn in its position in the ground as well as being photographed. But not so Schliemann. Here was treasure, and his one desire was to wrest it from the ground before the workmen spotted it. With his usual presence of mind, he knew exactly what to do. Although it was much too early, Schliemann sent all his men off to their quarters for breakfast, and then, as soon as they were out of sight, he began to dig with a large knife.

'This required great exertion,' he announced later, 'and involved great risk, since the wall of fortification, beneath which I had to dig, threatened every moment to fall down upon me. But the sight of so many objects, every one of which is of inestimable value to archaeology, made me reckless, and I never thought of any danger. It would, however, have been impossible for me to have removed the treasure without the help of my dear wife, who stood at my side, ready to pack the things I cut out into her shawl, and to carry them away.'

The treasure included various large objects of copper, vessels of silver and of gold, bronze lance-heads, battle-axes, double-edged daggers, and various other weapons. More important was the astonishing quantity of jewellery whose catalogue reads like something from the *Arabian Nights*. There were gold diadems, pendants, bracelets, fifty-six gold ear-rings and no fewer than '8,700 small gold rings, perforated prisms, dice, gold buttons, small perforated gold bars, small ear-rings, etc'.

When he first discovered it, Schliemann was convinced that the treasure had belonged to the household of King

Priam, and in evidence he recalled Homer's description of treasures in the palace, among which were chests containing all manner of precious objects ranging from textiles and jewellery to goblets and cauldrons.

Vividly, Schliemann reconstructed the last moments before his treasure's burial. 'Apparently someone in Priam's family', he wrote, 'had hastily packed away the treasure in boxes, which they had carried out without even taking time to remove the keys from the locks. Then, on the walls, this person met his death either directly at enemy hands or when struck down by a flying missile. The treasure lay where it fell, and presently was buried under five or six feet of ashes and stones from the adjacent royal house.'

Later, however, he rewrote the passage, carefully leaving out the references to Priam and to the royal house. But, in the first flush of success, Schliemann had no doubts. In search of more treasure he hastily enlarged the area of excavation, even pulling down one of his largest wooden houses in the process. Describing the results of these efforts he said, 'I found there many interesting antiquities, more especially three silver dishes, 1 foot 9 inches below the place where the Treasure was discovered: two of them were broken in pieces by the labourers' pickaxes, the third is entire. That the Treasure itself escaped injury from the pickaxes, was due to the large copper vessel, which protected it in such a way that I could cut everything out of the hard debris with a knife.'

As soon as the season's digging was completed, Schliemann set about smuggling his treasure out of the country for fear that the Turkish government might not approve of his going off with its national antiquities. Only when the gold was safely on its way did Schliemann let the story of the discovery leak out. When it did, the Turks were most displeased, and showed their displeasure by searching his house. But they, of course, found nothing. Legal action was then taken, the Turkish government claiming half of all the antiquities which had been found during the Troy excavations. The wrangle lasted a whole year and at the end of it, it was decided that Schliemann should pay Turkey the small sum of £400 in settlement of its claim. To a man of Schliemann's wealth this was but a drop in the ocean, and he was so delighted that he was prepared to be generous.

'Instead of £400,' he wrote, 'I sent in April 1875, £2,000 to the Turkish Minister of Public Instruction, for the benefit of the Imperial Museum, expressing my great desire always to remain on friendly terms with them, and explaining to them that they stood as much in need of a man like myself as I stood in need of them.'

Although the increased payment was readily accepted and Schliemann returned to Constantinople at the end of 1875, he found that the Turks were not sufficiently impressed to be willing for him to continue digging at Hissarlik. Later, in 1878-9, he was allowed to work for two further seasons, but although more finds were unearthed, Schliemann's great moment had passed. He had by this time transferred his attention to Mycenae, and still with the words of Homer ringing in his ears, he set about the ruined city in his own inimitable style. Here again his luck held, and once more he unearthed treasures which amazed and fascinated the newspaper-reading world. But that is another story.

When Heinrich Schliemann died at Christmas, 1890, his body was taken in state to Athens, were it was visited by the King of Greece, the resident diplomats, and all the great figures in classical archaeology. Silently they bade farewell to the man who had devoted so much to showing the world that all legends are not fiction. Sadly the great men uttered their inadequate words of sympathy to Schliemann's still beautiful widow and to his two children, whom he had named Andromache and Agamemnon.

Now, more than half a century later, we look back and perhaps sneer too readily at Schliemann and his methods. There is no doubt that for his time he was a great man.

It is true that in rushing in where experts feared to tread, he made many mistakes. But had he possessed a modern archaeological training, his energy, vision, and single-mindedness would surely have made him one of the greatest archaeologists of all time. It would be unfair to blame him for having lived too soon.

## CHAPTER FIVE

# THE CITY THAT VANISHED IN A DAY

If it were possible to take a great modern city and, without warning, plunge it into a deep freeze and then to keep it in ice for nigh on two thousand years, we should be creating conditions rather similar to those which brought about the death of the Roman city of Pompeii. The cars, the buses, and the trains would all draw to a standstill; the wheels of industry would cease to turn; the man in a restaurant would stop in the middle of his meal, the mother in the midst of her washing, and the children at their play. There they would remain until archaeologists came to thaw them out twenty centuries later. What, we may wonder, would these experts of the future make of us? Would they laugh at the things which we hold dear; pity us for our primitive way of life; or, perhaps, admire and envy us for the things that we, ourselves, do not appreciate?

Some of these thoughts must surely have crossed the mind of anyone who has been lucky enough to have visited Pompeii. There before them lies the life of a city, cut off in a single day and miraculously preserved for us to see.

The 24 August A.D. 79, dawned hot and sultry, and the inhabitants of the three towns of Pompeii, Herculaneum, and Stabeii yawned and stretched themselves in preparation to start a day which seemed likely to be just the same as every other day. Above them the crater of the volcano Vesuvius belched its familiar cloud of black smoke which drifted slowly out to sea, carried by the

Vesuvius burst open, bubbling up great mushrooms of smoke.

gentle salt breeze. Slaves were busily attending to their masters' needs; rich men wandered down to the baths, while women gossiped amongst themselves, discussing the latest scandal from the court at Rome and commenting on the colours of the fashionable new fabrics newly arrived from Alexandria.

Suddenly the towns shuddered under the force of a gigantic explosion as the top of Vesuvius burst open, hurling up a great mushroom of smoke which rose, multicoloured, into the sky like the creation of a nuclear scientist. The smoke rolled across the face of the sun, turning day into dusk, sending birds to roost, and the people to the protection of their household gods. At Herculaneum, which stood on the coast in the shadow of the mountain, a terrifying avalanche of mud, volcanic ash, and water came bowling through the town, filling the gutters, rising over the doorsteps of houses and shops, and flowing into the rooms. Terrified women and children splashed through the mire seeking safety wherever they thought it might be found. But all the time the thick, glutinous mud rose higher and higher, pouring now through windows, cascading like treacle down sloping, tiled roofs into the courtyards, burying everything in its path.

At Pompeii the scene was rather different, for it lay to the south side of the mountain and rather further away. Here there was no water, no mud; merely a gentle shower of volcanic ash which settled caressingly and silently like grey snowflakes. At first it was so light that the townsfolk may have been merely irritated by the way that it dirtied their freshly swept floors and settled on their courtyards, fountains, and statuary. But before long, events took a more sinister turn, for the gentle ash was supplemented by a rain of small volcanic pebbles which rattled like hail on the roofs, frightened the doves, sent dogs howling for shelter, and the people to shuttering their windows. From the mountain top came further shattering explosions and flashes of light, which lit up the pall of smoke until it seemed that the sky itself was afire. Thicker and faster fell the stones, accompanied from time to time by smoking lumps of pumice stone which made any sortie into the street a perilous venture.

By this time the populace realized that prayers to the gods would avail them little and that they would be advised to leave the town until the volcano had spent its force. Even now they still believed that they were experiencing nothing more lethal than the eruption of a minor volcanic cone. Families rounded up their valuables and loaded them onto carts, not because they expected never to see Pompeii again, but because they were afraid that thieves would break into their houses in their absence. But once in the narrow streets amid the falling stones panic quickly seized them. Carts piled up one behind another as they queued to pass through the city gates, and those at the rear cursed those in front who, in turn, shouted at the families and the carts ahead of them—and all the time the ash kept falling.

The air was full of sulphur fumes and everywhere the people were coughing and crying out for air. Panic gripped the town. The gates were blocked with fleeing carts and, seeing this, many people gave up the idea of leaving the town and ran back into their houses, covering their faces with their clothes to escape the fumes. But they were no safer indoors than out, for the yellow, choking fog was everywhere. Soon roofs began to collapse under the weight of volcanic stones. One by one, crushed or choked, the people of Pompeii died.

All day and into the night the volcano continued to hurl its stones and ash into the sky and to disgorge fiery ribbons of molten lava down its slopes. By morning the nightmare was over. The sun shone down from a cloudless sky and the mountain expelled nothing more dangerous than a thin wisp of smoke which curled into the heavens like the trail from a cigarette. But on its slopes and over the land at its foot, smoke and steam still rose from the cooling pumice and lava. Here and there, blackened, leafless trees were still smouldering, and from the safety of neighbouring hills came the wind-borne cries of surviving Pompeians mourning their dead. Of the three towns, Pompeii, Herculaneum, and Stabeii, there was no sign. It was as though they had never been.

The buried towns were destined to sleep undisturbed for nearly seventeen hundred years. It was not until Queen Maria Amalia Christine, consort of Charles de Bourbon, inquired as to the origin of certain pieces of statuary in the palace garden at Naples that any interest was taken in the historic sites. The statues, it seemed, had been accidentally unearthed at Herculaneum and so, to amuse the queen, a Spanish military engineer was instructed to start digging there in the hope of finding more treasures. This proved to be easier said than done, for the town was covered by more than 49 feet of rock-hard lava which could only be chipped by exploding gunpowder. Nevertheless, the Spaniard persevered, and after blasting his way through the lava his workmen found themselves (although they did not know it) on the stage of the theatre, where they came upon a mass of fallen statuary. The figures had stood in niches or on pedestals at the rear of the stage, and when the back wall had been struck by the rolling wave of lava they had toppled forward and crashed down to lie where the workmen found them. Soon after these discoveries had been made an inscribed stone was recovered which identified both the town and the theatre by name.

As the work progressed, the Spaniard's treasure-hunting instincts were subdued by the presence of the royal librarian, who imparted to the engineer a genuine interest in acquiring information as well as portable treasures. Being heartily sick of battling with tons of unyielding lava, he decided to move his scene of operations to the other side of the mountain, to Pompeii, a site which seemed likely to offer much easier digging.

Work started at the beginning of April 1748, and only a week later the first house walls complete with mural

Here were the first human remains to be found in Pompeii—
a man lying face down still clutching a handful of coins.

paintings had been unearthed, along with the first human remains—those of a man lying face down still clutching a handful of coins. But after making these dramatic discoveries the excavators filled in their holes and returned to Herculaneum. The reason for their departure is not clear; but it is possible that the king declared himself to be more concerned with acquiring statues for his queen than in digging up human bones.

In 1754, digging began again in Pompeii, digging which developed into the systematic excavation of a large area of the city. This started in earnest in 1763 and has continued more or less without interruption until the present day. During the early nineteenth century the work was sponsored by the French government and subsequently by the reigning Bourbon monarchs. In 1861, the Italian government took control and has retained it ever since. Today, more than two-thirds of the city have been cleared and every season new finds continue to be made.

The first town on the site of Imperial Pompeii dates as far back as the sixth century B.C., when the prevailing political and artistic influence was Greek. Towards the end of the fifth century B.C. the town was seized by the warlike Samnites, and later, during Rome's wars with these people, it was occupied by the Romans. Later still, in 80 B.C., Pompeii became a Roman colony and so entered into its final phase. In A.D. 63, the city was badly shaken by an earthquake. Then, after being quickly rebuilt, it stood to await its death blow, which was to come only sixteen years later.

Although some of those who escaped returned soon after the disaster to dig for possessions and the bodies of their loved ones, it is fair to claim that when archaeological excavations began all was virtually as it was on that day in August A.D. 79. All that remained of the bodies of fleeing Pompeians was found heaped at the gate which opened on to the road to Herculaneum, trapped in the congestion and laid low by the weight of the possessions which they had refused to leave behind. Here were two women crouching with their clothing held across their faces to escape the fumes, while in a nearby house a group of mourners were discovered still seated at a funeral feast. Animals, too, were found, both beasts of burden and household pets. Among the latter was a domestic guard-dog still with a chain and collar around its neck. Chickens were found in their runs, pigs in their sties, bread in the ovens, and wine on the tables.

The shops of the silversmiths, blacksmiths, dyers, bakers, were all there—complete with the tools and products of the trades. In the taverns money was still on the tables where it had been hurriedly set down by departing guests. The great wine jars remained in serried ranks waiting for the customers who would never return, while on the tavern walls were scrawled verses and the names of girls—put there by young men in love.

The Pompeians were apparently addicted to writing and drawing on walls and consequently innumerable inscriptions (*graffiti*) are to be found throughout the city. Curses, caricatures, school lessons, mathematical problems, political slogans, advertisements for shows in the amphitheatre, all are there. Few of these inscriptions can claim any artistic merit. For this the visitor must turn to another aspect of the Pompeian legacy—to the painted walls and mosaics of the houses. Here we may gaze on the greatest collection of ancient art ever assembled. In shops one finds painted scenes illustrating the activities of the owners' trades and crafts, while private houses contain panels depicting legends and religious rituals. Elsewhere are painted scenes in architectural perspective and others in formal garden designs showing flowers, birds, and fountains. The designs of the mosaic floors vary as much as do the painted walls. While many of the patterns are coldly but beautifully geometric, others portray fishes, beasts, and legendary figures. Among the most dramatic mosaics are those which show chained and snarling guard-dogs—a warning to visitors to beware of the dog. In case the meaning should not be sufficiently clear, one craftsman even worked the Latin words 'Cave Canem' into his design!

Although some of the finer wall paintings have been removed to the safety of the National Museum at Naples, as also have the most precious objects recovered during the long years of excavation, much still remains in the original buildings. Many more relics grace the cases of a museum in the city, among them casts in clay of some of the people who died in the disaster. These remarkable but pathetic exhibits were made possible by the fact that the volcanic ash falling over the victims solidified like plaster of Paris, thus faithfully preserving the shape of clothing and features of the dead people. When the archaeologist's trowel reached the remains he would find a cavity in the ash which often represented a mould for a complete human figure. By carefully pouring plaster or liquid clay into the cavity, leaving it to set, and then chipping the ash from around it, he was left with a moulded replica of the dead person, preserved in every detail.

There have, of course, been innumerable great moments in the history of the excavations at Pompeii. But the project as a whole unquestionably stands as the greatest discovery in the story of Roman archaeology. No truly great names are associated with it, but all those who have taken part in the work, from the convicts employed by Charles de Bourbon to the highly skilled Italian archaeologists of the 1950's, have all contributed to the wonders that we can see today. Specialists in many fields—architects, artists, dress designers—all can and do gain inspiration from the discoveries at Pompeii. But the great majority of the visitors who go there have no specialized interest. They are there merely to enjoy the unique experience of walking the streets, visiting the homes, shops, and temples—rubbing shoulders with the ghosts of the people who watched the grey snow fall on that tragic summer day in A.D. 79.

## CHAPTER SIX

# A TEMPLE IN THE LIMELIGHT

THE laying bare of the public and private life of a whole town during the excavations at Pompeii did not mean that the last word has been said in Roman archaeology. Astounding though the discoveries were, they could tell us nothing of life in the Roman Empire after A.D. 79, nor can they be used as an unvarying guide to the pattern of Roman provincial communities. In Britain, archaeologists must seek their own Pompeii. Needless to say, they will never find it, and so they must be content to make do with the scattered scraps of evidence which are so painstakingly gathered from innumerable sites up and down the country.

Every year since the close of the second World War, London has been the scene of continuous archaeological activity. There, for the first and last time, excavators have been able to investigate the fantastically rich soil which lies beneath the city. It has often been claimed that it is impossible to dig anywhere within the City walls without unearthing relics of one sort or another. This is no exaggeration, and every day building excavation uncovers new treasures. Two-thirds of them are invariably lost, having been hauled out by mechanical diggers and tossed unnoticed into the waiting lorries. Of those that are spotted in time, some disappear into the pockets of the finders, to be sold later to collectors and tourists, while the remainder reach the safety of the City's Guildhall Museum, where they are repaired and later exhibited to the public.

The staff of Guildhall Museum is responsible for

watching the builders' excavations so as to recover and record anything that may turn up. It might be a wood-lined Roman well, a mediaeval rubbish pit, or the floor of a house destroyed in the Great Fire of 1666. The date makes no difference, for these things are all part of the story of London; the relics of the seventeenth or eighteenth century receive as much care and attention as those that may be two thousand years old.

Deliberate archaeological excavations are carried out in the City under the auspices of the Roman and Mediaeval London Excavation Council whose director, Mr (later Professor) W. F. Grimes, played so important a part in the recovery of the Sutton Hoo Treasure (Chapter Eight). The Council and the city's museum work hand in hand, the latter being responsible for the preservation of all the objects recovered during the excavations. These bald facts may not seem particularly interesting or even to have any bearing upon archaeological great moments. Nevertheless, they are important in that they provide a key to all the varying work which has been accomplished since the war.

When we realize that the ground level of the City has, in places, risen more than 20 feet since the Romans first settled there, it is understandable that to dig through that accumulation is a long and exacting task. Not only is it difficult; it is also extremely expensive. It is therefore only possible to explore thoroughly a minute section of the total area. This constantly raises the question of 'Where can we dig to the greatest advantage?' It is no use shutting one's eyes and stabbing at the map with a pin. Each site has to be chosen with the greatest care, every trench being dug with the intention of finding the answer to some specific problem. But even when the archaeologists know from measurements or earlier discoveries roughly where to look, they are still frequently disappointed. Modern concrete foundations may prove too thick to be breached without mechanical aid or they may find that the Roman gateway or piece of wall which they seek had been destroyed in mediaeval times. On the other hand the excavation may reveal something totally unexpected. Even in these days of modern scientific archaeological methods luck still plays its vital part.

The Roman city of Londinium stood on two gravel hills on the north bank of the river Thames, hills which represented the first point at which incoming ships could unload their cargoes onto dry land. Further downstream the river was flanked by dangerous and inhospitable marshland. Between the hills which are now known as Ludgate Hill (on which stands St Paul's Cathedral) and Cornhill, a stream once ran and was known as the Walbrook. Although one can see nothing of it today, a narrow street which runs down towards the Thames from the Mansion House to Cannon Street Station still bears that name.

Whenever building excavations have been carried out in the valley between Ludgate Hill and Cornhill an astonishing number of fine Roman relics have been recovered from a thick deposit of black, peat-like silt. Professional and amateur antiquaries who watched these excavations during the nineteenth century firmly believed that the black 'peat' represented the bed of the lost river Walbrook. At a point directly to the west of Cannon Street Station the deposit was found to be no less than 248 feet in width. Here, they thought, once flowed a river broad enough for sea-going ships to sail up it into the very heart of the city. This exciting theory was supported by the discovery, near the Mansion House, of what was claimed to be a barge laden with ancient grain. On the strength of these discoveries romantic minds envisaged the Roman Walbrook flanked by warehouses and wharves teeming with merchants and piled high with merchandise imported from the far corners of the Empire. They saw the river itself partially obscured by a mass of hulls and the gaily painted sails of galleys from Ostia, Tyre, and Alexandria. Fragments of tile flooring found in the valley were labelled as the remains of wharves, while a roughly hewn block of stone unearthed in 1949 was hailed by the press as a bollard to which Roman ships were once moored. The fact that the stone was quite the wrong shape passed without comment.

Excavations carried out for the foundations of St Swithin's House on the east of the Walbrook street succeeded in exposing part of the black silt deposit, and it was during this work that the so-called 'bollard' was found. The digging was watched by the staff of Guildhall Museum, and a number of discoveries were made which caused some doubt as to whether the 'peat' really did represent part of the old river bed. The floors and foundations of houses built in the second century A.D. were found to overlie the silt, and objects found in the black deposit could be dated late in the first century A..D This factor indicated that the 'peat' had been laid down or was in a fluid state until a few years before the houses were built. On this evidence one had to assume either that the Walbrook river suddenly dried up or was moved into a new channel or that the silt had never formed part of the river bed. If the latter theory were to be accepted, two puzzling questions were posed. What did the 'peat' represent and where was the true bed of the river?

In an attempt to answer these questions the Roman and Mediaeval London Excavation Council resolved to excavate on a large bombed site to the west of the Walbrook street and opposite the newly erected St Swithin's House. Although the bombs had destroyed a vast area, the choice of a spot in which to dig was strictly limited, for the majority of the old basements and cellars were still filled with brick rubble which could not be moved. There was, in fact, only one cellar running east-west across the possible line of the river which was not choked with debris. This, therefore, was the point at which excavating began in 1952.

No sooner had the modern concrete flooring been removed than Mr W. F. Grimes was confronted with the remains of a substantial Roman building which lay directly beneath it. The structure was of basilican form, having a curved or apsidal western end, and had possessed a roof supported on two rows of seven columns which divided the interior into a nave and two aisles. At this early stage only the northern half of the building was exposed, the remainder still lying beneath the foundations, walls, and rubble of the bombed modern offices. The north wall of the Roman building was coated with plaster and painted in gay colours, while the floor was of pink mortar and was overlaid here and there by heaps of broken tiles. The few fragments of pottery found among them indicated that the building had been abandoned during the fourth century A.D.; but the quality of the construction indicated that it had been built much earlier.

The discovery of the Roman building was naturally exciting, but it certainly did not solve the problem of the Walbrook river. Like those under St Swithin's House, this structure had been erected over, and its foundations sunk into, the well-known black silt. The river itself would therefore have to lie beneath the narrow strip of ground covered by the modern street or alternatively follow some course west of the curving end of the Roman building.

Sticking firmly to his original plan, Mr Grimes resolved to suspend work on the newly found building and to continue his search for the Walbrook. New trenches were cut to the west of the apse and in them his labourers worked at great depths often up to their knees in water. As they cut down through foot after foot of the black silt they unearthed many a fascinating relic of Roman London, among them pewter plates, candlesticks of brass and lead, the blade of a small sword, as well as a group of objects beautifully fashioned in ebony.

After months of digging the sandy bed of a stream was located under the black 'peat' at a depth of between 32 and 35 feet below the modern street level. But this was no ship-carrying river, merely a timber-revetted watercourse no more than 14 feet in width.

While the investigation of the stream was still in progress it became known that the builders would shortly be moving onto the site in preparation for laying the foundations of Bucklersbury House, London's first sky-scraper. The Roman building still awaited attention and time was running short. At about this time, amateur helpers working for Mr Grimes uncovered two large pieces of stone which were lying within the area of the building. The first turned out to be an uninscribed altar, while the second was found to be lying face down and when turned over proved to be part of a carved relief showing a male figure carrying a burning torch which he was holding downwards. This was clearly part of a figure of Cautopates, who represented night and was an attendant of the god Mithras. Another find was a small male torso in marble, and these relics, coupled with the church-like plan of the building, indicated that the excavators had accidentally stumbled on a Roman temple.

While Mr Grimes and his colleagues were hurrying back through the soil of time the builders were equally busily preparing for the future. Temporary offices and hoardings were springing up on the site, and pneumatic drills and bulldozers were already being used to clear and dismantle cellars in the vicinity of the temple. The contractors, realizing the importance of the Roman discoveries, came to the rescue of the archaeologists and carefully removed the modern debris which covered the remaining concealed portions of the temple, thus giving Mr Grimes a chance to record almost the entire plan of the structure. Eventually, however, the builders came to the conclusion that the presence of the archaeologists and their temple was impeding the wheels of progress. Consequently the excavators were given a date by which time their work was to end.

This deadline fell on a Monday, and on the preceding Friday a newspaper reporter visited the site in search of a story. Believing that no report could reach the public until after the site had been vacated the archaeologists gladly answered the reporter's questions. But sensing a scoop the newspaperman raced back to his office in time to push the story into the Saturday edition.

Although the news of the discovery was carried by only one Saturday newspaper large numbers of people made their way to the site to see the temple before it was destroyed—so, too, did many newspaper correspondents. Visitors clambered over the walls, carrying off fragments of tile as souvenirs, reporters tried to obtain interviews with the excavators, and all around cameras were clicking and flash bulbs popping. In the midst of this chaos the archaeologists worked steadily on. Suddenly, at the eastern end of the temple, a workman unearthed a sculptured marble head which was at once recognized as that of the god Mithras.

By the following morning the press had turned the god into a household name, and ere the day was out all the world and his wife was *en route* for the Mansion House in the hope of catching a glimpse of the relics. The hour of destruction grew steadily nearer and the mechanical diggers stood ready with their gleaming jaws agape waiting for the word which would send them clawing and biting into the temple walls. But Monday dawned, and the order never came. The company which owned the site had decided to allow the archaeologists more time, and so the builders' hand was stayed.

The next step was to make it possible for the thousands of people who still wanted to see the remains to be given access to the site. Barriers were accordingly erected, explanatory notices set up, and police detailed off to control the crowd. Meanwhile, the newspapers were whipping the discovery into a nine-day wonder. The headlines proclaimed 'The Mithras Mystery', 'Mithras Conquers London', and 'Big New Find at Temple', then '15,000 at Roman Temple', '30,000 See Roman Temple', 'Crowd Breaks Through Roman Temple Barrier' and 'Roman Temple Crowd Clash With Police'. The queues of sightseers wound through the City streets—hundreds upon hundreds of people all waiting to see they knew not what.

The marble head of Serapis, the Egyptian god of the harvest, found on the site of the Mithras Temple in London. He has a corn-measure on his head.

Less than a week later more statuary was unearthed at a point close to the spot where the head of Mithras had been found. This time there were two marble heads, one of Minerva and the other of the corn god Serapis. With them lay a beautifully sculptured statuette of Mercury seated on a ram, along with a giant marble hand holding the hilt of a dagger. All these objects, as well as pottery and a stone bowl, had been buried in front of the wooden steps just inside the temple doorway and had clearly been put there for safety—perhaps to prevent their being destroyed by the Christians. These dramatic finds naturally added fuel to the fire, so that the world's press was abuzz with the name of Mithras to an extent unequalled since the discovery of Tutankhamen.

By this time the public outcry had reached astonishing proportions and streams of letters reached the newspapers demanding that the temple should be preserved for all time. Architects were called upon to estimate the cost of preserving it and they eventually decided that forty or fifty thousand pounds would be needed. The great question then was—who will pay? The Minister of Works, Sir David Eccles, had visited the site and it was he who encouraged the site owners to let Mr Grimes continue, but his Ministry could not produce the vast sum of money to ensure the temple's permanent preservation. As anxious days passed rumour after rumour circulated in the city, some people saying that the Prime Minister himself would visit the site and order the builders to save the ruins, while others said that the Corporation of London would provide the necessary money. Neither rumour proved to be founded on truth.

Eventually, the Legenland Trust, the site owners, offered to defray the cost of removing the temple stone by stone and re-erecting it in the forecourt of the new building. While this offer was readily accepted, it proved to present one major snag, this being that the stones would have to be stored on another vacant site until the work on Bucklersbury House was completed. Once the plan was accepted, the builders surged hungrily forward even though the archaeological excavations were still far from completed. While trowels, teaspoons, and soft brushes were still removing the soil inch by inch from the eastern end of the temple, the picks, shovels, and pneumatic drills of the builders' labourers were crashing and boring into the western extremity, the stone and tiles from the temple walls being thrown into buckets and carried away to their temporary home. On arrival they were laid out in the rough plan of the original temple, but when the workmen found that they had a mountain of pieces over, they heaped them in a great pile in the middle where they soon became an attraction for souvenir hunters. Subsequently a wire fence was erected to protect them, thus preserving the historic stones from the hands of human vandals but leaving them to the weeds, the rain, and the frost.

Meanwhile, back on the site, a workman's pick had smashed through as yet unexamined soil and had shattered a priceless group of marble figures. Fortunately most of the fragments were salvaged and when pieced together made up a single unit representing the god Bacchus standing beneath a grape vine and accompanied by his aged nurse, Silenus, seated on a donkey, and by a figure of Pan, a leopard, and two attendants. Unhappily, only the goat-like legs of Pan survived, while the heads of both attendants were lost. Roughly carved on the base of the group was an inscription which has been translated as meaning 'Long life to wandering men'. Various other fragmentary inscriptions were found in and around the temple, one of them being discovered by a thirteen-year-old boy and his sister who had visited the site soon after the first news of it appeared in the papers.

When, eventually, the last of the temple had been hauled away to its temporary resting place, the foundations which were too deep to move were left to the mercy of the mechanical grabs, so too were most of the timber features from the inside of the building. Before long there was nothing but a deep, water-filled hole to mark the place where London's most sensational discovery had stood.

Although future generations of Londoners will be unable to gaze upon the spot where the rites of Mithras were practised in the city, much has been salvaged and will survive to serve as a reminder both of the temple and of the work of Professor Grimes and his colleagues. Not only will students be able to read his inch-by-inch account of the excavation, but they and the curious public will still be able to see the temple's sculptured treasures in the galleries of Guildhall Museum.

Once the builders had removed the temple from their path the machines tore into the soil in an attempt to make up for lost time. The builders may even have hoped that the speed of their work would have prevented any further archaeological finds from being made. Throughout these operations the staff of Guildhall Museum had the unenviable task of salvaging what it could from the very teeth of the grabs

Previous building excavations in the 'peat' of the Walbrook valley had unearthed a staggering number of metal, leather, and wooden antiquities—objects which could only survive under the special conditions provided by the black silt. Mr Grimes's deep cuttings west of the temple had shown that similar discoveries were likely to be made on this site and the archaeologists were confident that more treasures would be found before the builders' digging was completed.

No sooner had the first teeth gouged into the silt than quantities of pottery and leather objects began to be found. Delicately worked sandals lay beside heavy, hob-nailed boot soles, fine glass was found crushed under fragments of coarse, pottery *amphorae*, and thin bronze needles rubbed shoulders with rough iron nails. Pieces of wooden planking, stakes driven into the ground, and carpenters' trimmings were everywhere—preserved just as perfectly as on the day that they first came to rest in the ground.

As the days passed, more and more objects went pouring

into the museum laboratory—all of them crying out for immediate attention. The wood, if left to dry naturally, would have twisted and warped, while the leather threatened to shrink to a fraction of its original size if it were not treated at once. Luckily, the technical staff had had experience of preserving similar waterlogged relics and it knew exactly what to do. The wood was impregnated with liquid alum, while the leather was restored to its original suppleness by immersion in special castor oil baths.

Every day, important wooden structures and innumerable other relics were swept relentlessly away by the grabs. Deeper and deeper they bit into the ground until, eventually, they reached a point some 30 feet below the existing street. At this level the builders began to drive concrete piles and to dig a series of trenches and pits to receive their reinforced foundations. No sooner had this work begun than rows of oak piles began to be uncovered. These ran in two uneven lines, 8 to 15 feet apart, on a north-to-south line at right-angles to the course of the river Thames. Filling the area between the rows lay a thick deposit of black silt topping three or more layers of water-washed sand. When the labourers began to dig into these sandy strata they discovered to their astonishment that they were laden with Roman metal objects of every imaginable description. The museum archaeologists realized that the men were digging into the true bed of the Walbrook, a section of which had been exposed during Mr Grimes's excavations.

Again the builders were approached in the hope that they might delay the clearance of the Walbrook bed until the relics could be recovered. But no respite was forthcoming. The past, they said, must give way to the future. Consequently the archaeologists were only able to operate when the machines and labourers were not working and thus two-thirds of the unique relics were lost. Nevertheless, an astonishing number of finds were saved. In one afternoon's work more than a hundredweight of Roman metal

An artist's impression of the rites practised in the temples of Mithras.

(*After a drawing by Alex Sorrell*).

objects was retrieved. Thousands of iron nails were salvaged, and with them lengths of iron chain, knives, chisels, hammer-heads, keys, pick-heads, trowels, shackles, bale-handling hooks, punches, ox-goads as well as innumerable unidentified objects. The majority of these finds were in such a remarkable state of preservation that they could still serve their original purposes.

A chisel found by one of the workmen was taken home and sharpened on a mechanical grinding-wheel. When it was eventually handed over to the museum the tool possessed so sharp an edge that it could be and, indeed, was used to chisel a modern piece of wood. A similar story can be told of a large iron hook which was found by a workman and used on a modern pile-driver, where it was in constant use lifting a weight of more than five tons for more than a fortnight. The hook might have still served this purpose to this day had it not been pointed out to the archaeologist. After being retrieved it was found to have suffered no ill effects save for a slight rubbing of the surface—such was the preserving power of the Walbrook silt.

While the iron objects were the most plentiful, there were many others of bronze, copper, pewter, lead, and even of gold. Among them were decorative hair-pins, brooches, ear-rings and finger-rings, needles, surgical instruments as well as small spoons, tweezers, and manicure sets. Other finds included bronze folding foot-rules, decorative chair fittings, brass hinges, and small brass plates identical with those that we still use to hang bathroom mirrors today. Of particular interest was a small group of letters made of brass and with nails at their backs so that they could be hammered into wood. These, too, are paralleled today by the metal letters which one can buy to affix to a garden gate to tell tradesmen to 'Beware of the Dog' or to inform the world that this is the entrance to 'The Nook' or 'Mon Repos'. We can only guess at the way in which the Roman letters were used, but they could quite well have been employed to put an owner's name on a chest or a door.

It was the realization that all these objects could be mistaken for their modern counterparts that made the Walbrook discoveries so sensational. One's astonishment at finding that there seemed to be nothing new under the sun seemed to oust the almost inevitable thrill of discovery. There was no time for careful excavation. It was simply a matter of digging and sifting as much silt as possible in the shortest time. The stream bed still ran with draining water, and so whenever a hole was dug it immediately became filled. The only method to adopt was to dig down beneath the water level and then feel about with one's hand for the familiar shapes of man-made objects. Up came the finds as fast as hands could grasp them, the bronze and brass gleaming like gold in the sunlight. There were no problems of corrosion; everything emerged as bright and shining as the day it was made.

The builders' labourers were not idle, for while the archaeologists worked, they too were digging, recovering tools, jewellery, and nails by the handful. By night, amateur treasure-hunters descended onto the site cutting great holes in the banks of builders' trenches in their search for loot.

The contractors were naturally becoming more and more sorry that archaeologists had ever been allowed on the site, and they began to lay the crimes of the amateur treasure-seekers at the door of the professionals. Before long machines had almost entirely replaced the hand-digging and it was now no longer possible to sift through the silt as it was dug out. If the finds could be given a price, it would be true to say that a fortune was being tipped into the ever-waiting lorries and carried off to the soil dumps where the treasures, robbed of their air-excluding silt, would quickly corrode away.

While we cannot help but mourn over what was lost, there is much for which to be grateful. Through the generosity of the landowners Guildhall Museum acquired a collection of Roman finds unequalled anywhere else in Britain.

Although the building and archaeological excavations on the site of Bucklersbury House provided many new facts about Roman London, many new questions were posed. The most pressing of these was the problem of how all these metal objects came to be lost into the stream bed. Gone was the theory that the Walbrook was once a great anchorage into which the shipping of the Roman world brought its merchandise. Nowhere on the site was the Walbrook found to be more than 14 feet wide and at its narrowest it did not exceed 8 feet. The objects could not, therefore, have been lost when being loaded or unloaded onto the Walbrook's wharves. What, then, was the answer?

A clue to part of the mystery was provided by the discovery that a number of the metal finds were unfinished and that the silt had also yielded a quantity of iron slag, drops of lead, and bronze trimmings—all suggesting that metal-workers had been operating in the vicinity. But although the finds may have come from that source, it would still not explain why so many complete, new, and unbroken objects had found their way into the water, nor would it account for the presence of more than eighty first and second century Roman coins which were scattered here and there through the silt.

The archaeological evidence indicated that towards the end of the second century the revetted walls of the Walbrook were allowed to fall into disrepair, many of the timbers having fallen forward into the stream. As a result the water strayed away from its prescribed course and eventually flooded back across the valley, flowing in small channels more or less as it liked. It may be that we shall never learn the full story of the Walbrook, for where once the stream flowed and the temple of Mithras proudly stood now rises Bucklersbury House, its walls towering high into the sky and its foundations thrusting 50 to 60 feet into the ground. Nevertheless, there still remain a few small areas between the great concrete blocks and piles where the Walbrook silt lies undisturbed and still clutches in its sandy grasp a few of the treasures of Roman London. When, one day in the distant future, Bucklersbury House makes way for another building, a new generation of archaeologists will experience the same thrill of discovery that we felt in 1955.

*CHAPTER SEVEN*

# MEN BENEATH THE SEA

It was a day in June, 1943, when a trio of Frenchmen hurried to a secluded cove on the French Riviera and proceeded to unpack a strange piece of apparatus. Had the Italian occupation troops been watching, they would at once have seized the contraption, believing it to be a secret weapon. But they would have been wrong, for the leader of the group was Commander Jacques-Yves Cousteau, and the curious cylinders were part of the first 'aqualung' underwater breathing apparatus which he had just invented. Within ten years the name of the man and his invention would be known the world over. But on this day, by the shore of the blue Mediterranean, the 'aqualung' was an unknown gadget and was being tested for the first time.

With the three air cylinders strapped to his back, the mask over his face and the two tubes looping over his head and running to the mouthpiece between his lips, Cousteau resembled some fantastic visitor from outer space. Slowly and crab-like, he made his way down to the water, staggering under the fifty pounds of weight on his back. But once beneath the surface the weight vanished and he was free to breathe and fly like a bird through the blue sky that was the sea.

'I thought of the helmet diver,' he wrote later, 'arriving where I was in his ponderous boots and struggling to walk a few yards. . . . I had seen him leaning dangerously forward to make a step, clamped in heavier pressure at the ankles than the head, a cripple in an alien land. From this day forward we would swim across miles of country no man had known, free and level, with our flesh feeling what the fish scales know.'

When Homer was writing the *Iliad*, divers were plunging into the Mediterranean in search of treasure—treasure in the form of sponges. Ever since those remote times man has been trying to conquer the undersea world, spurred on not by the desire merely to enjoy the thrill of movement beneath the waves, but to seize from it the treasures which lie in Davy Jones's locker. From the time that man first ventured on to the sea in ships, storms and reefs have taken their toll. The merchantmen of Greece and Tyre, the galleys of Rome, the galleons of Spain, and the great steel vessels of the twentieth century are all represented among the wrecks which lie scattered beneath the oceans of the world. Many of them still contain precious cargoes which salvage companies would give their right arms to recover.

Urged on by the thought of the treasures that would be theirs if only they could reach beneath the sea, inventors toiled through the centuries to create a diving suit that would enable men to work and breathe on the sea bed. But even when man did learn how to reach the bottom and live, he was still bound hand and foot by weights, life-lines, and breathing tubes—a leaden puppet on priceless strings.

No sooner had reasonably effective diving equipment been produced than men sank bravely down in a stream of bubbles in the hope of finding a treasure which would make the risk worth while. Sometimes they were in luck beyond their wildest dreams, and they tore the treasure ships apart in their quest for bullion and saleable relics. No one pretended that this was archaeology. It was treasure-hunting pure and simple, but in the eyes of contemporary antiquaries it was justifiable. They reasoned that if the objects were not brought to the surface in this way they would never be found at all. There were no skilled archaeologists who would be prepared to encase

Almost immediately the diver located a heap of shattered wine jars lying on the sea bed.

themselves in canvas, lead, and copper and conduct excavations on the sea bed. Even if they had been forthcoming, the equipment was such that they would have been unable to achieve any more than could the professional diver.

With the advent of the 'aqualung' the picture immediately changed, for it was now possible for undersea excavators to move as they wished, to squat down and gently scrape with a trowel or to dig with a spade if the need arose. The principles of archaeological observation, excavation, and recording could now be transferred—with modifications—to the bed of the sea. No longer does a diver need to be in the peak of physical condition before entering the water. Today, anyone at practically any age can don an 'aqualung' and become an undersea explorer.

As long ago as the second century A.D. the writer Pausanias recalled that 'Fishermen of Methymna, having cast their nets into the sea, drew them in and discovered a head carved from the wood of the olive tree'. Ever since that time fishermen and sponge-divers working in the waters of the Mediterranean have brought to light a never-ending flow of relics from long-forgotten shipwrecks. It is not surprising, therefore, that Commander Cousteau should soon have set his sights in this direction.

Following a report that a quantity of Greek *amphorae* had been located in 60 feet of water, Cousteau took his research ship the *Élie Monnier* to the site and almost immediately located a heap of shattered wine jars lying on the sandy bottom. They almost certainly represented part of the deck cargo of a Greek merchantman whose hull lay buried in the mud and sand beneath them. Using a powerful suction pump a shaft was cut into the silt in the hope of locating the vessel, and from the hole came a hundred or more amphorae, some of them with their stoppers still in place and sealed with wax impressed with the initials of ancient wine merchants. These seals were later examined by scholars and identified as those of

A Greek merchantman of 2,000 years ago. Divers found the hull of a ship like this and part of its cargo on the sea bed of the Mediterranean.

Marcus and Caius Lassius, a family established both in Pompeii and Sorrento in the second century B.C.

'For several days we siphoned mud and *amphoras*', wrote Cousteau in his book *The Silent World*. 'Fifteen feet down we struck wood, the deck planking of a freighter. . . . We were not equipped to carry out full-scale salvage and our time was limited. We went away with *amphoras*, specimens of wood, and the knowledge of a unique hydro-archaeological site which awaits relatively simple excavation. We believe the hull is preserved and could be raised in one piece. What things that wreck might tell of the ship-building and international commerce of the distant past!'

In 1950, the same year that Commander Cousteau was

busy on the site of the wreck off the Balise de la Chrétienne, Italians were investigating another lying in much deeper water off the Ligurian port of Albenga. The famous salvage ship the *Artiglio*, which had brought up the *Egypt's* gold in 1932, was here brought into play. Conventional divers were sent down at a spot where fishermen had trawled up quantities of pottery and they too found innumerable *amphorae*, many of them unbroken. But there was no sign of the ship whence they came. The hull, if it survived, presumably lay deep in the sand. It was proposed, therefore, that a giant grab should be lowered from the *Artiglio* which would bite into the sea bed, cutting a deep trench across the suspected line of the ancient hull. The mud and sand caught between the jaws would then be hauled to the surface for examination. This plan was considered acceptable and work was soon under way. In less than two weeks of digging the grab tore right through the wreck and brought to the surface no fewer than 728 *amphorae*, but of these only 110 were intact. The work was then abandoned. The whole project was far from being an essay in archaeological technique; but it must be excused on the grounds that the wreck lay in water too deep for 'aqualung' divers. On the other hand it might be argued that man will eventually conquer the pressure barrier and be able to work carefully and scientifically at greater depths than is now possible, in which case the wreck would have been better left to rest a little longer in peace.

The thrill of investigating wrecks is not to be enjoyed only within the Mediterranean—although, of course, there are probably greater discoveries to be made there than anywhere else. In America, the blue lagoons of the Caribbean lure both museum officials and amateur treasure-hunters on holiday. There, amid the coral reefs, lie the wrecks of ships of the seventeenth and eighteenth centuries, ships which flew the flags of Britain, Spain, France, or the Jolly Roger of the buccaneers. Further north in the mouth of the York River in Chesapeake Bay rest the remains of British ships sunk during the siege of

Yorktown in 1781, some of whose fittings have been recovered and now grace the showcases of the Mariners Museum at Newport News in Virginia.

British waters are, unfortunately, ill-suited for undersea research; although the rocky shores of Scotland, Wales, and the West Country have taken more than their fair share of the world's shipping. Dangerous currents and the muddiness of the water successfully protect most of the more promising wreck sites. In Tobermory Bay, off the Isle of Mull, lies the almost legendary *Francesca*, the pay-ship of the Spanish Armada. But although repeated efforts have been made to salvage the fortune which is reputed to lie in her holds, all have failed. Near Hope Cove on the south Devonshire coast lies the wreck of another Armada vessel, a fact which is brought to the notice of the local inhabitants after heavy storms, for there, washed up on the beach, they find Spanish doubloons and pieces-of-eight. A much older wreck lies off the coast of Kent, resting, so it is believed, on Pudding Pan Rock. The ship was a Roman merchantman bringing red Gaulish pottery (Samian Ware) to Britain in about A.D. 140. For centuries dishes and bowls have been washed ashore near Whitstable, where they have been used by the villagers in their kitchens. In the present century conventionally attired divers have been sent down to search for the wreck. But although they found scattered sherds of pottery, they saw no sign of the ship. In 1955 and 1956 'aqualung' divers tried their luck, but fared no better, and it is generally believed that the hull will never be located. However, the long-dead captain might rest more easily in his grave if he were to know that at least some of his cargo did reach Britain and that more than forty dishes, bowls, and cups are to be seen in the British Museum—a distinction which they might never have achieved had the Pudding Pan ship reached port.

The story of undersea archaeology is only just beginning and it is probable that for years to come scientific investigation will continue to be confused with treasure-hunting. In truth there has as yet been no single great moment of archaeological achievement in this watery field. Commander Cousteau and his colleagues do not pretend to be archaeologists; but their researches into the use and development of underwater equipment have paved the way for the submarine scholars of the future.

## CHAPTER EIGHT

# SENSATION AT SUTTON HOO

DIGGING holes in ancient burial mounds, or *tumuli*, has long been a favourite sport of English landed gentry. Victorian clergymen would happily open two or three before breakfast, robbing the skeletons of their possessions and carrying them triumphantly home to display in the rectory cabinets. Happily, that time is now past and the tumulus-diggers of today are no longer educated vandals but serious archaeologists. Nevertheless, if one were lucky enough to own land which sported two or three ancient mounds, there would naturally be a great temptation to find out what they contained. It so happened that the late Mrs E. M. Pretty was in just this position, for she owned a large estate at Sutton Hoo, near Woodbridge, and on it stood no fewer than eleven burial mounds of varying sizes.

After much careful consideration Mrs Pretty decided that she would investigate at least some of the mounds. But she was no vandal, and so to ensure that the work was undertaken correctly she arranged for the excavation to be supervised by Mr Guy Maynard, the curator of Ipswich Museum, while the actual digging was carried out under the direction of a Mr Basil Brown.

The first mound to be opened proved to have suffered at the hands of grave-robbers, and so contained nothing. A second had been similarly treated, although it was possible to detect the rotted outline of a boat, 18 feet in length, which had been buried beneath the mound. The third tumulus proved more rewarding, and in it the excavators found two cremated, human burials, a burnt and fused glass bowl, a disc and button of gilt-bronze, as well as part of a late Roman stone plaque which also showed signs of burning. It was deduced that all these things had been placed in the funeral pyre and that after the flames had died down the remains were salvaged, placed on a long wooden tray (traces of which could still be seen) and laid to rest in a shallow grave over which was heaped a mound of turf and sand.

To Mrs Pretty, the finds from the first summer's excavations were more encouraging than satisfying, and she decided that next year her workmen should tackle one of the larger mounds. Accordingly, in July, 1939, work began again, once more under the direction of Messrs Brown and Maynard. The tumulus chosen did not seem particularly promising, in spite of its size, for there were definite signs that someone had been there already. The mound was oval in shape and it was decided that the best method of attack would be to slice it down through the middle. Digging began at the east end, and almost as soon as they started the excavators encountered the brown lines of decayed wood and the rusted heads of iron clench nails. Remembering the boat which had been found during the previous year, Mr Brown was convinced that he had stumbled on another, though larger, boat which protruded beyond the end of the mound. He immediately stopped digging into the vessel itself and concentrated on carefully removing the mound which overlaid it.

It is almost impossible to keep a major archaeological discovery a secret and the Sutton Hoo find was no exception. A request to another museum for information regarding Viking boats soon caused other archaeologists to wonder what was afoot. Consequently Mr Maynard received a visit from the well-known antiquary, Mr C. W. Phillips. When the latter was taken to the site and saw the partially exposed boat he realized that here was a find of the greatest importance. He prevailed upon Mrs Pretty to call a halt until experts from the British Museum and the Ministry of Works could reach the site. Subsequently Phillips himself was invited to take control of the excavation on behalf of the Ministry, and this he gladly agreed to do. Later he enlisted the services of Professor Stuart Piggott and his wife, Mr J. B. Ward Perkins, who has since become Director of the British School at Rome, Mr (afterwards Dr) O. G. S. Crawford, and Mr W. F. Grimes, now Professor Grimes and famous for his discovery of London's Mithraic temple.

As the 9-feet high mound was carefully removed it became painfully obvious that early suspicions had been well founded. Grave-robbers had been at work and had dug a large hole down into the middle at a point where the burial might be expected to lie. But luckily, the treasure-hunters had abandoned their efforts without finding anything. After going down 9 feet they stopped, had a meal in the hole, and then filled it in again. The evidence for the meal took the form of a number of animal bones, a heap of wood ash, and part of a pottery jug dating from the late sixteenth or early seventeenth century. Although it is popularly accepted that the robbers actually ate in the hole, it certainly seems odd that only one fragment of the jug should have been found. It could, perhaps, be argued that the meal was eaten on the top of the mound and that the refuse was shovelled into the hole afterwards, while the rest of the broken jug was thrown away into the nearby bushes. The problem is, in this case, completely unimportant; but it is typical of the hundred and one riddles which face every archaeologist on practically every excavation.

We do not know why the robbers decided to stop work. They may, perhaps, have been afraid that the sides of their hole would fall in on them or they may even have believed that they had, in fact, reached the bottom. However, we do know why they failed to find the burial. As Mr Brown, the excavator, found in 1939 the boat lay in a trench below the present ground level, but extended some

The outline of the Sutton Hoo burial ship could only be distinguished by the rows of nails which had held the wood together and by the imprint the planks had left in the sand.

13 feet eastward beyond the limit of the mound. This had come about as a result of mediaeval ploughing which had cut away the end of the tumulus. The robbers, being unaware of this, dug down through the centre of the surviving section of the mound and so were well away from their goal.

When Mr Phillips took over the excavation on 10 July 1939, the eastern half of the boat had already been exposed, and amidships could be seen traces of a collapsed timber structure which was almost certainly part of a burial chamber. It was decided that the latter should be investigated first. So it was that while the storm clouds of war were gathering in Europe the sun shone down on the little group of archaeologists as they laboured carefully on at Sutton Hoo; brushes, trowels, and tablespoons being their chosen weapons for this attack upon the sands of time. As the work progressed it became apparent that the burial chamber had been a little more than 17 feet in length, and had had a gabled roof whose lower edges rested inside the gunwales of the boat. So, when the weight of the mound had been laid on top of it, the pressure bearing down on the roof had gradually forced the sides of the vessel outwards. The final collapse of the burial-chamber's roof had caused a great quantity of the mound material to sink down onto anything that may have lain inside.

When, at last, the collapsed sand and turf had been scraped away the excavators realized—if they had not already done so—that they were not dealing with a Viking ship but with a Saxon burial dating from the seventh century A.D. As each shovelful of sand was brushed away so the edges of metal objects began to protrude like rocks amid a yellow sea. Here were lumps of brown rust, there the green of corroded bronze, and here again the yellow gleam of gold and the ruby richness of inlaid garnets.

At the eastern end of the burial-chamber lay the corroded remains of three bronze cauldrons and an iron-bound, wooden bucket. Beside the cauldrons was found a quantity of iron chains, rings, and bars which, although too decayed to be safely identified, may have formed some kind of gear for suspending the vessels.

At the western end of the chamber were discovered the distorted remnants of a wooden shield which was at first thought to have been a tray. The shield's large iron boss was topped by an ornamental disc and was decorated in gilt-bronze, while the wood of the shield itself was adorned with the figure of a bird of prey fashioned in bronze, plaster coated with gold leaf, and with garnet inlay. Also attached to the wood was another figure, this time a dragon in beautifully worked gilt-bronze. Beside

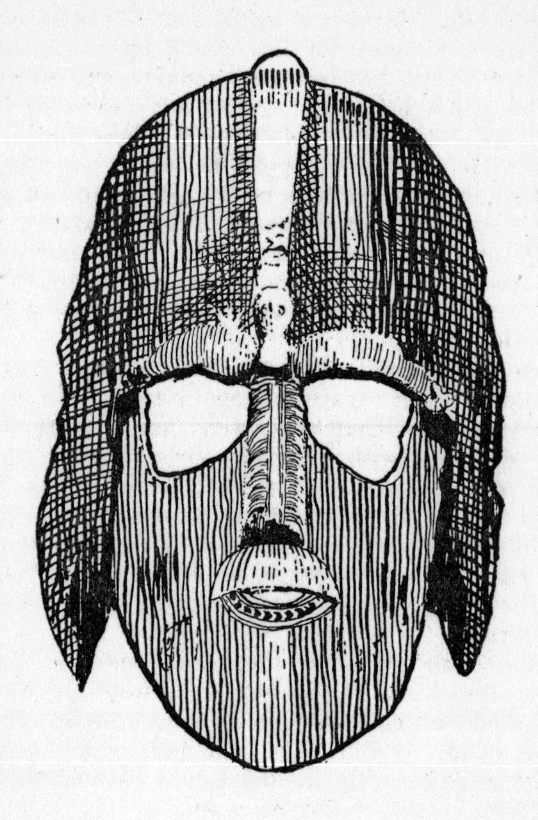

Among the Sutton Hoo treasure was this iron helmet decorated with bronze, gilt, and silver. It was found in hundreds of pieces, which had to be fitted together.

the shield lay a large, ornamental whetstone weighing more than 6 pounds, which was presumably used for ceremonial purposes, perhaps symbolizing the mastery of the sword. Next to the whetstone was found a large iron standard with a spike at the bottom for thrusting into the ground and with a beautifully made bronze stag decorating the top. Beside the standard head were found the remains of another bucket, and beyond it a cluster of iron spear-heads whose wooden shafts had completely rotted away. However, it was possible to see that the spears had been about 7 feet long, for their iron ferrules still marked the place where the shafts ended. The only other objects at this, the western end, of the chamber, were two bronze bowls lying one inside the other.

The groups of finds from either end of the chamber formed as it were, the ends of an 'H', for the remainder of the treasure was distributed along the east-west line of the boat, thus forming the cross-bar of the letter. At the western end lay the almost unrecognizable remains of an iron helmet decorated with bronze, gilt-bronze, and silver, while near by was a nest of nine silver bowls set one inside another. Under the bowls were found two silver spoons inscribed with the names Saul and Paul in Greek letters—spoons which may have been used in Christian baptism. Close by was discovered the rusted remains of a magnificent sword with a hilt and pommel of jewelled gold. Scattered around it lay a group of gold buckles, clasps, and ornaments, all decorated with garnets and mosaic glass.

Next to the sword was found one of the most informative of all the objects in the burial-chamber; it was a purse, or rather the gold and jewelled lid of a purse, for the bag itself had rotted, leaving no trace. Not so the contents; under the lid were found thirty-seven gold coins, three gold blanks rubbed smooth for minting into new coins, and two small gold strips. The coins are considered by leading experts to have been put into the purse at some time after A.D. 650 and probably before about A.D. 670.

Thus, on this evidence, it is possible to set the date of the burial to within twenty years.

In the centre of the burial-chamber was found a group of silver-mounted drinking-horns. These, it seemed, had originally been wrapped in cloth, a few fragments of which still survived. Beyond the horns lay a huge silver dish measuring 27 inches in diameter and bearing stamps showing that it had been made within the Byzantine Empire during the reign of the Emperor Anastasius (A.D. 491-518). Consequently this wonderful find has come to be known as the 'Anastasius Dish' although, of course, it never actually belonged to the emperor.

When, eventually, the great dish was carefully removed, the surprised excavators discovered that it had served only as a lid to cover many more remarkable objects. Among them were a bowl, cup, and ladle of silver, six cups made from gourds with gilt-bronze rims, two hanging-bowls, two bone combs, a horn cup, the remains of a leather bag and shoes, and finally the rusted remnants of a coat of mail. All these things had been laid out on a wooden tray. Close to the great silver dish was found the least impressive of the Sutton Hoo treasures, a simple pottery bottle, plain and unadorned. Lastly, away from the main areas of objects and against the south wall of the chamber was located the remains of a third bucket.

This was the extent of the Sutton Hoo Treasure. It may seem a little puny when compared with the wonders, say, of the tomb of Tutankhamen. Nevertheless, it constituted the richest grave ever found in Britain, and in its own way it can claim to be of greater archaeological importance than the Egyptian treasure. The Sutton Hoo finds told the story of a ritual unparalleled before in this country, whereas the ceremony of ancient Egyptian burial was already well-known when the tomb of Tutankhamen was discovered.

All those experts who were privileged to examine the Sutton Hoo finds were agreed that many of the gold objects were unique in Saxon archaeology. But it did not require the knowledge of an expert to realize that one very important object was missing from the burial. Where, everyone asked, were the bones of the great man to whom the treasure belonged? Here were the weapons, the armour, the family heirlooms, all the trappings needed to send him safely on the road to Valhalla, the palace of immortality where the souls of warriors lived for ever. But of the man himself there was no sign. It was clear from the layout of the treasure that it had never surrounded or covered an inhumated body. This was not particularly astounding, for it was quite reasonable to expect that the warrior would have been cremated and his ashes placed in an urn which, in its turn, would have been put in the centre of the burial-chamber. But there proved to be no such urn nor even a single fragment of charred, grey bone.

In attempting to find the explanation for the absence of human remains, we must first consider the clues revealed by the excavation. The splendour of the treasure clearly indicates that the deceased was a man of high rank and almost certainly a king. The coins point to his having died between the years A.D. 650 and 670. Furthermore, the fact that the boat contained the man's wordly goods indicate that this was a pagan and not a Christian burial. However, it would seem from some of the objects, notably the silver spoons, that he had Christian associations. Lastly the absence of the body may indicate that the king was drowned at sea or died on some distant battlefield where his corpse was unrecognizable or could not be retrieved.

Although many experts refuse to commit themselves, others have suggested that Aethelhere, King of East Anglia, was the most likely candidate to fulfil all the requirements. Although he had a Christian wife (who left him to become a nun), it would seem that he was not himself a Christian, for he allied himself with the pagan king of Mercia in the latter's war against Christian Northumbria. Aethelhere eventually died at the battle of Winwaed in Yorkshire where, according to the Venerable

Bede, more warriors were drowned in floods than in the fighting. The battle occurred in the November of A.D. 655, and so the death of Aethelhere fits very well between the dates put forward by the coin experts. Assuming that it would take some time for news of the king's death to reach East Anglia, it may be deduced that the cenotaph ship—for that is what it was—was made ready early in A.D. 656.

So much public attention was lavished upon the Sutton Hoo treasure that only the archaeologists showed much interest in the great boat. This is, of course, perfectly understandable, for nothing remained of the boat but the stains where timbers had rested and the sand-embedded clench nails which had once held them together. Compared with Viking ship-burials found in Denmark and Norway, the Sutton Hoo vessel was a pathetic shadow of its former self and one which could never be transferred to a museum. Nevertheless, as a result of brilliant excavating, it was possible to reconstruct, on paper, practically every detail of its structure.

The boat was 89 feet in length and 15 feet wide amidships and was clearly already old when it was buried, for there was evidence that it had been substantially repaired during its seagoing life. There was no depth to the keel and it is thought that it had neither sails nor mast, but was rowed by thirty-eight oarsmen and steered from the stern by a large paddle. Nautical experts who examined the remains could find no trace of any internal fittings, but they concluded that the seating and stern deck where the helmsman stood had all been stripped out before burial. There was no doubt, however, that the boat had been a full-scale, seagoing vessel. How, we may wonder, did it come to be buried on the crest of a windswept escarpment seven miles inland from the coast? The accepted answer is that it was rowed up the river Deben to within half a mile of the site and was then hauled on rollers up the 100-foot incline to the Sutton Hoo heathland, where a specially dug trench awaited it. Then, supported on ropes passed beneath the keel, it was gently and evenly lowered into the ground. Only then was the burial-chamber constructed and the treasure laid out inside. When, at last, the ritual of burial had been completed, the sand from the trench was poured back into the gap between the boat's timbers and the grave's sides, and also into the ship itself, thus sealing the clinker-built hull in a solid bed of sand.

The last of the treasure had been removed from the burial-chamber on the 29 July 1939, but much work still remained to be done on the clearance of the bows and stern of the boat. The precious finds had, therefore, been taken for safe keeping to the British Museum in London. But as always happens when objects of gold or silver are unearthed, a Coroner's inquest had to be called to decide the ownership of the finds.

The ancient and unwritten law of 'finding's keeping' has no place in the English code. Archaeological finds made in this country normally belong to the owner of the land where they are unearthed, but when they are of bullion (gold or silver) the Coroner may claim them for the Crown under the law of Treasure Trove. This law states that if the objects were hidden by someone who intended later to retrieve them then they are still his property and must be handed over to his descendants. While that may be possible in the case, say, of a box of guineas hidden in a cottage chimney, there is rarely any way of tracing the owner of an archaeological discovery. So, when no owner can be found the gold or silver is seized by the Crown and handed over to the Treasury. In mediaeval times the bullion was melted down and turned into coins, but nowadays the Crown realizes that the archaeological value of the finds may be greater than their value as precious metal and so the Treasury passes them to another government office—the British Museum. The museum then pays the finder the full market value of the objects; so there is never any question of his being the loser through being honest!

That, however, is only one side of the law of Treasure

Trove; the other says that if the objects have been lost, thrown away, or have been buried without any intention of retrieving them, then they are said to have been returned to the common stock and become the property of the finder. In some cases this is disputed when the finder is not the owner of the land. But at Sutton Hoo this state of affairs would not arise, for Mrs Pretty was both landowner and instigator of the excavation.

On the 14 August, the Sutton Hoo Treasures were brought back from the British Museum under armed escort and laid out in the village hall at Sutton where the inquest was to be held. There, before a jury of twelve Suffolk householders the Coroner listened to the story of the discovery as it was told by the experts who had taken part in the excavation. But the inquest was little more than a formality, for the verdict was already a foregone conclusion. The people who had placed the precious objects in the burial chamber had had no intention of ever retrieving them and so they could not be claimed by the Crown as Treasure Trove. The Sutton Hoo Treasure was therefore declared to be the property of Mrs Pretty, and she would have been quite within her rights to have bundled the whole lot into a suitcase and taken it home to ornament her mantelpiece.

When the verdict was reached there must have been many people who, not knowing Mrs Pretty, wondered what would become of the precious relics. Many of the objects were in so fragile a condition that even Mr Phillips and his colleagues were loath to handle them, and the thought of their being turned over to unskilled hands was almost unbearable. Even supposing that the new owner would be prepared to sell the treasure, its value had been placed so high—running into a giant six-figure sum—that no one could imagine where sufficient money could be found to pay for it. But as it turned out, there was no cause for alarm. In an astonishing act of generosity and public spirit Mrs Pretty gave the entire treasure to the nation. Mr Phillips has since described it as the greatest gift ever made to the National Collection in the lifetime of a donor.

As a result of this wise and magnificent gesture the dishes, bowls, cups, drinking-horns, helmet, sword, shield, and all the other finds were carefully deposited in the laboratory of the British Museum. But by this time the scent of war was strongly in the air. Volunteers were filling sandbags in the parks, and in every home householders were testing their black-out curtains and trying on their gas-masks. The sense of urgency and impending danger had even filtered through the staid portals of the British Museum. Officials were busily packing up the finest treasures and making them ready for storage in the comparative safety of a disused underground station. This was hardly the moment for the arrival of what the museum had since described as 'the most marvellous find in the archaeological annals of England'. Nevertheless, the laboratory staff rose magnificently to the occasion, administering first aid to those objects most needing it, making an inventory of all the finds, and then packing them so that they could survive in storage for the duration of the war.

The packing of the Sutton Hoo Treasure proved to be one of the final tasks performed by the laboratory staff before war was declared. It was fitting, therefore, that six years later the unpacking of it should be one of its first peace-time duties. In view of the difficulty and importance of the work that had to be done the laboratory staff was increased to deal with it. Visitors seeing the Sutton Hoo Treasure today can have little idea of the fantastic jigsaw of almost shapeless pieces which faced the restorers. The piecing together of the helmet alone took one expert six months of continuous work. Nevertheless, when the British Museum again opened its doors in 1946 the greater part of the Sutton Hoo Treasure was waiting in the cases to astound the first visitors. As far as the public was concerned, the story of Sutton Hoo was over; but for archaeologists years of research still lay ahead.

Away on the escarpment above the river Deben the empty tumulus is still to be seen—along with its ten companions. The experts believe that the group represents nothing less than a Saxon royal cemetery. We may wonder, therefore, what treasures might yet lie beneath the remaining, unopened mounds. Perhaps, in years to come, Sutton Hoo will again burst into the headlines, to add another golden page to the story of British archaeology.

*CHAPTER NINE*

# THE WELL OF THE RAIN GOD

IN 1879 a schoolboy wrote an article entitled 'Atlantis not a Myth', and to his slight surprise it was accepted and published in the American magazine *Popular Science Monthly*. In the article he suggested that the Maya culture of Central America was an off-shoot from the civilization which once existed on the drowned continent of Atlantis which, according to legend, had vanished in a day and a night beneath the waters of the Atlantic Ocean. The article, as its author later admitted, contained many a rash statement; but it caused a minor sensation at the time. The boy's name was Edward Herbert Thompson, and as a result of his article it was remembered when the American Antiquarian Society was looking for someone who could investigate a group of Maya ruins in the Yucatan peninsula.

Although Thompson had had no experience of excavating or of the country, his enthusiasm won him the job. The President of the United States appointed him to the post of an American Consul in Mexico and made him responsible for the states of Yucatan and Campeche. He was told that all available time should be spent not in the stuffy consular office but in exploring the ruins of Yucatan. So, with his wife and two-month-old baby, the youngest consul in the Mexican service set out to begin his life amid the jungles and mangrove swamps of that country's southern states.

When Thompson began his career as consul and archaeologist, American antiquaries had given little thought to the archaeology of their own continent. While they would willingly spend time and money on sites in the Middle East, they chose to ignore the civilizations which lay buried under their own doorsteps. Yet the ancient peoples of Central America, the Toltecs, the Maya, and the Aztecs, were, in their own way, just as fascinating as the Egyptians, Babylonians, or Assyrians. It is true that the American cultures were not as old, but their buildings, rituals, and artistic talent were a match for anything to be found in the Old World.

The story of the Mayan civilization begins at some unknown date prior to A.D. 374, during which phase the people settled in western Honduras and in northern Guatemala. Here they built their cities of stone and concrete on plains which are today covered by uninhabited jungle. Towards the end of the sixth century A.D. they ceased building and it is thought that they soon abandoned the sites and moved away northward into the Yucatan peninsula to build another empire. This lasted until the arrival of the Spaniards in 1526, by which time their civilization was in a decline. Centuries of warring with their neighbours had hastened the process and had resulted in the absorption of foreign cultures, notably that of the Maya's northern neighbours, the Toltecs. The dawn of the sixteenth century found the Maya in no state to withstand the armoured conquerors of Catholic Spain and within a generation a thousand years of greatness was swept away.

At first the Spaniards tried to take over the Maya sacred capital of Chichen Itza as their seat of government; but the inhabitants resisted so fiercely that the idea was abandoned. The conquerors therefore retreated to the town of T'ho, and made that the administrative centre of the new province, renaming it Merida.

It was to Merida that Edward Thompson was sent when first he took up his post of consul. From there he began a series of exploratory sorties which took him to most of the great Maya sites. But although they each

A great stone mass pierced the sky, crowned by a temple.

yielded up their relics, there was one site to which Thompson returned again and again—the fabulous sacred city of Chichen Itza. In his book *People of the Serpent* he tells how, after a long and dangerous trek through the jungle, he first caught sight of the lost city.

'The gradual ascent,' he wrote, 'and winding of the trail between the boulders and the big trees seemed so like familiar forest rambles at home that it came over me, almost with a shock, that the boulders I passed by so carelessly had cut surfaces and were once carved columns and sculptured pillars. Then, just as I began to understand that the level, forest-covered surface beneath my feet was a terrace made by ancient man, I peered up to a great stone mass that pierced the sky, and all else was forgotten. A pyramid with terraced sides, panelled walls of cut limestone, and broad stairways leading upward, was crowned by a temple. Other buildings, high mounds, and broken terraces, were buried in the forest, and only the dark green knobs on the horizon told where they stood.'

Thompson was spell-bound. It was one of the most exciting moments of his life. 'Pen cannot describe', he wrote, 'or brush portray the strange feelings produced by the beating of the tropic sun against the ash-coloured walls of those venerable structures. Old and cold, furrowed by time, and haggard, imposing, and impassive, they rear their rugged masses above the surrounding level and are beyond description.'

He knew that here was his destiny, and he there and then resolved to dedicate his life to the excavation of this one site. But although the vow was made, fulfilment of it was still some years away. Although he returned to his beloved city many times in the interim, he always had other more pressing work to do. It was during one of his return visits that Thompson noticed a long mound of tumbled masonry different in character from the rest of the ruins around him and he asked his native companion what it might be.

'It doesn't look like the ruin of a Maya building', he added.

'You are right, Don Eduardo', his friend replied. 'It is all that is left of what was once the big plantation house.' Then he went on to tell how the plantation had been destroyed and the house burnt by rebels in 1847. As he listened to the story a great idea came to Thompson.

'As I gazed upon those shapeless heaps of toppled walls and jungle tangle and noted the fertility of the soil and the luxuriant forest that rose in solid masses behind it, an inspiration came to me. I would purchase the old plantation, rebuild the houses, plant the fields, fill the corrals with fine cattle, and from the sale of crops, stock, and timber, finance my scientific ventures.'

All this Thompson did, and in buying the 100-square-mile plantation he not only obtained the ground on which to grow crops and make money for his excavations, he also acquired the city of Chichen Itza itself. This was the stuff of which dreams are made, for every archaeologist would give his right hand to have been in Thompson's shoes—having the capital of a lost civilization in his own back garden. He could dig where he liked, when he liked, and for as long as he liked, without anyone being able to interfere.

Comparisons are always dangerous, but it might be fair to compare Thompson with Heinrich Schliemann, the discoverer of Troy. Schliemann, you remember, had pinned all his faith in the words of Homer and had triumphed regardless of the scoffers who looked upon the *Iliad* as a mere fairy tale. Thompson, too, had his Homer in the shape of one Diego de Landa, who had been the Spanish Bishop of Yucatan during the third quarter of the sixteenth century. The bishop wrote a long account of the customs of his heathen flock, and in it he had a deal to say concerning Chichen Itza. Thompson had first read the account when preparing his youthful article on Lost Atlantis, and he believed every word of it. While friends scoffed, he declared that De Landa would lead him to the city, and, sure enough, he did.

One passage in the bishop's story excited the antiquary more than any other. It told how a wide and handsome road led away from the great pyramid temple towards a deep well.

'Into this well,' wrote De Landa, 'they have had and still have the custom of throwing men alive as a sacrifice to their gods in time of drought, and they believed they would not die, though they never saw them again. They also threw into it many other things like precious stones and things they prized, and so if this country had possessed gold it would be this well that would have the greater part of it, so great is the devotion that the Indians show for it.'

When Thompson reached Chichen Itza he found a level terrace at the base of the pyramid temple, and from it a causeway, 25 feet in width, extended north for about 300 yards. There, at the end of it, just as the bishop had said, was the sacred well.

It was not really a well as we understand the word, for this was a natural hole in the limestone, 187 feet across at its greatest width. The edges were obscured by a tangle of overhanging trees and jungle creepers, and 60 feet below the rim lay a sheet of dark, forbidding water. The limestone walls above it had been much eroded, and from its ridges and miniature caves all kinds of tropical plants hung down towards the water. Some of the holes were used as homes by the many snakes which sunned themselves on the ledges or lay camouflaged amid the hanging creepers. Further down, on a level with the surface of the water, a shelf jutted out and on it grew a clump of balsa-wood trees.

'The interlacing roots of these strange trees,' wrote Thompson, 'half buried in the black mould about them and half-showing, darkly smooth and shining, seem like the writhing bodies of antediluvian reptiles. In the moist and darkly shadowed places beneath them can be seen the glistening eyes of giant toads, turtles, and lizards. This little beach is like a scene from the time when the world was young.'

Somewhere in the silt at the bottom of this pit Thompson believed that he would find a treasure which would make archaeological history. De Landa's account had not let him down yet. Why should it do so now? Besides, there was a second description of the ritual of the sacred well, and where there was so much smoke, there surely, must be fire.

The second story of the well had been written in 1579 by Don Diego Sarmiento de Figueroa, the Alcalde, or mayor, of the district wherein Chichen Itza lay. It appeared in an official report to Charles V, the King of Spain, and in it the sacred pit was described as the *Cenote*. The account told how, after sixty days of fasting, the Maya lords arrived at the edge of the well and threw into it women selected from their households, telling them to beg favours for their masters from the gods who dwelt at the bottom.

'The women,' wrote the mayor, 'being thrown in unbound, fell into the water with great force and noise. At high noon those that could cried out loudly and ropes were let down to them. After the women came up, half dead, fires were built around them and copal incense was burned before them.'

When the unfortunate women had recovered, they told their masters that they had seen many of their own people lurking in the deep shadows below them and these people had told how the noble lords would fare in the coming year. This story, fantastic though it may seem, was to be of the greatest value to Thompson when he eventually followed the Indian maidens into the depths of the sacred well.

No sooner had the archaeologist taken up residence on his newly acquired plantation than he began to toy with the idea of plumbing the black depths of the *Cenote*. He knew that the bottom would be covered by many feet of

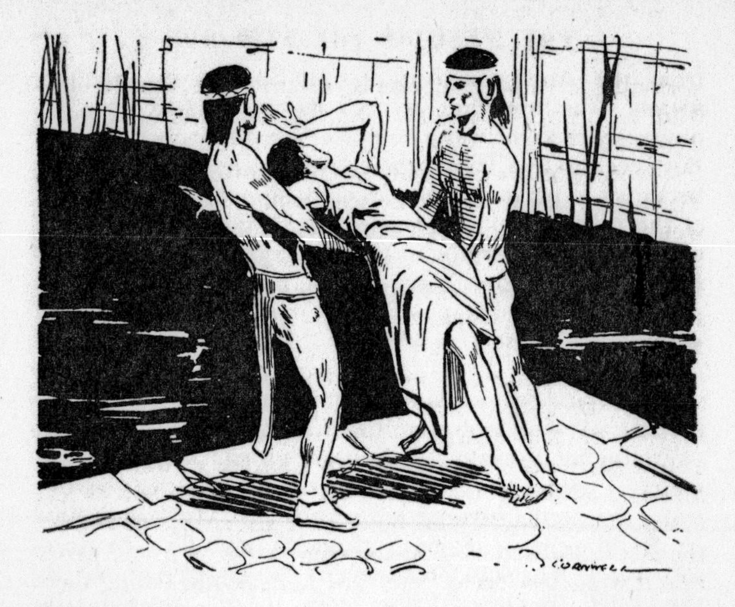

The Maya lords ordered the women to be thrown into the well.

silt and that it would cost a small fortune to clear it all out. But the longer he considered the problem the more certain he became that he would only need to excavate one section of the silt to recover all the treasures which might or might not have been thrown into it.

Thompson reasoned that the offerings to the well gods would have been thrown into the water from the end of the causeway and from nowhere else. Accordingly, he cut logs of the correct weight and shape, attached ropes to them, and threw them from the causeway into the well. He then measured the length of rope paid out, and from these calculations he decided just how far a sacrificial victim could have been thrown.

Thompson's next step was to approach the man who had first sent him to Yucatan, in the hope of raising funds from the American Antiquarian Society. At first the society was reluctant to be associated with what it obviously thought was a completely hare-brained scheme. But, eventually, Thompson's enthusiasm won the members over to his side and the society agreed to provide part of the money that was needed. With the backing of this august body, Thompson had little difficulty in urging Harvard University to provide the rest. He now returned in triumph to Yucatan with the money in his pocket and with ropes, hawsers, tackle, and a fine new dredge in his baggage.

Once back on his plantation, Thompson set to work in earnest. A working platform and derrick were set up overhanging the well, and down on the surface of the water a pontoon was firmly moored. Then, for the first time, the dredge swung out from the platform and, with its gleaming jaws agape, it plunged down into the deep, still water. The hawser slackened as the dredge reached the silted bottom. Then, after a few interminable moments, the winch began to turn, drawing up the dredge and in it, perhaps, the treasures of the lords of Chichen Itza.

'The water,' said Thompson, 'until then still as an obsidian mirror, began to surge and boil around the cable and continued to do so long after the bucket, its tightly closed jaws dripping clear water, had risen, slowly but steadily, up to the rim of the pit. Swinging around by the boom, the dredge deposited on the planked receiving platform a cartload of dark brown material, wood punk, dead leaves, broken branches and other debris; then it swung back and hung, poised, ready to seek another load.'

Down and up. Down and up. Day after day the jaws plunged into the abyss, and on the side of the well the mounds of decaying, organic silt grew higher and higher, while the stench became ever stronger as the steam rose from the drying heaps. But not a hint of treasure was to be seen. From time to time a handful of potsherds dropped from the dredge, and on one occasion it brought up the bones of a jaguar, relics of some recent jungle tragedy. With the passing of each fruitless day Thompson became more and more discouraged.

'Is it possible,' he asked himself, 'that I have let my friends into all this expense and exposed myself to a world of ridicule only to prove, what many have contended, that these traditions are simply old tales, tales without any foundation in fact?'

As each load of silt was added to the putrid heap his spirits sank lower and lower. Then, one day, it seemed that his luck might turn. That day, he said, was as grey as his thoughts as he plodded through the dampness to where he could hear the clicking of the dredge brake. He stood listlessly watching his brown-skinned workmen as they toiled at the winches. When, once again, the dredge broke surface he hardly bothered to glance down at it. But as it rose upwards his eye was caught by two yellowish, globular masses which protruded from the slimy mud. As soon as the jaws deposited their load Thompson seized the objects. They were made from some hard, waxy substance. Excitedly he broke a piece from one of the lumps and tasted it. It was resin. He next placed the fragment in the embers of a fire and almost at once a sweet, fragrant, smell rose up. Thompson remembered the story of the Indian maidens and how, after being dragged from the well, fires had been lighted and copal incense burnt before them. These lumps, he reasoned, must either be the remains of that incense or votive offerings to the well gods. That night, for the first time in weeks, the archaeologist slept long and soundly.

Although Thompson was, by this time, a tough, practical explorer with years of rugged experience behind him, he was still an archaeological romantic ready to pin his faith on the slenderest of clues. So it was with his lumps of resin. These, he was convinced, were to be the beginning of success.

'For a long time,' he wrote, 'the belief had been growing

in my mind that the scientific exploration of this sacred well of Chichen Itza was to be the crowning event of my life-work, and that to do it as it should be done, I must give it all my time and attention. With the finding of those two nodules of incense and the realization of what they indicated, this belief became a certainty. After much reflection I resigned my position as consul and devoted myself entirely to the work.'

He could so easily have been wrong. The incense need have been nothing more significant than an accidental loss, the sort of thing one expects to find in any well. If this were so, Thompson would have thrown up his job for nothing. But as it turned out, luck was on his side.

No sooner had he resumed his dredging operations than the treasures he sought began to come up with every load. Pottery vessels, temple vases, and incense-burners, arrow and lance-heads, axes and hammers worked in flint and calcite, all came up one after another. Among the hundreds of other finds were copper chisels, discs of beaten copper engraved and embossed with figures of Maya gods, and figures carved in jade. Here, too, were objects of gold, among them a variety of bells, discs, and pendant figures. Equally important among the discoveries were the salvaged skeletons of young women and of thick-skulled, low-browed men. These, Thompson concluded, were the remains of male human sacrifices and of the young women who had failed to return from their ordeal. He was satisfied that the writings of Bishop de Landa and Don Diego Sarmiento had proved to be true in nearly every detail.

One feature of Don Diego's account could hardly have been accepted by Thompson. Indeed, the Spaniard himself only professed to be reporting what the Indians believed. This was the passage in which he described how the maidens emerged from the water and claimed to have talked with the people that they had seen in the shadows beneath the surface. Although Thompson had given the story some thought, he had been confident that there was no logical explanation on which the legend could be based. Here he was wrong.

One day, while sitting in his pontoon on the surface of the well, Thompson was idly peering down into the dark water when suddenly he realized that the darkness was not as black as first it seemed. As he looked more intently he found that he could, in fact, see a series of deeps and hollows. Then, to his astonishment, he began to see human faces and hear the murmur of their voices—just as the Mayan women had claimed. But this phenomenon had a simple explanation. The deeps and hollows were really the reflections of the miniature caves which pitted the limestone walls of the pit, while the murmuring faces were no more than the reflections of his own workmen as they peered down from above. This, then, was the answer. The luckless women had seen the reflected heads of the Mayan priests and nobles as they bent over the abyss waiting for tidings from their gods.

After months of dredging, the metal jaws began to bring up nothing but recently fallen twigs and chips of limestone. The bottom had been reached. But although the grab had cut a hole right through the silt, it had by no means cleared all the contents of the well. Thompson had known from the outset that the machine's usefulness would be limited and it was for this reason that he had travelled to Boston to take lessons in deep-sea diving. Now, encased in canvas suit, iron-shod boots, and leaden collar, he was almost ready to descend into the depths himself. His native workmen shook him gravely by the hand, for none ever expected to see him again. They all believed that the well was inhabited by giant snakes and by fearsome, indescribable monsters.

Thompson was not worried. It was true that he had encountered large snakes and lizards swimming on the surface. But he knew that these had only fallen from their homes in the rock face and were more frightened of him than he was of them. At last the large copper helmet was screwed over his head and then, accompanied by a

The modern, copper-headed monster rose from the depths for the last time.

Greek professional diver, he sank beneath the surface. Down through the darkening water he went, down into the hole cut by the dredge until, at a depth of about 80 feet, his boots finally touched the bottom. In the thick, murky water his lamp proved useless, and he soon discovered that his telephone was more hampering than helpful. As he felt around the silt walls of his prison he could detect the shapes of innumerable relics which were still gripped by the mud. There was no sign of the giant snakes nor of the indescribable monsters.

Thompson estimated that the total depth of water and silt was about 65 feet, the first 30 feet of the latter being a soft mud thick enough to support roots and tree branches, while the lower levels were solid enough to imprison fallen columns and wall-stones. It was this lower deposit which he described as his 'fertile zone' and from which he recovered all the antiquities.

The work of extracting the plums from this muddy pudding was largely uneventful, although, from time to time, stones dislodged from higher up would fall on to the divers, luckily without causing any injuries. At long last Thompson was satisfied that no further treasures were to be found, and so the modern copper-headed monster rose from the depths for the last time.

When the American archaeologist had bought the Chichen Itza plantation he had seen it as a centre for archaeological and botanical research. He believed that, as news of his discoveries spread, he would be able to bring to Yucatan a thriving tourist industry, the sightseers being accommodated in hostels built on his land. The income from this source would then be used to further his researches. But these things were not to be.

Central America is traditionally a breeding-ground for anarchists and revolutionaries, and it was during one of the many local insurrections that Communist-inspired agitators urged their followers in Yucatan to burn the property of rich planters. So, while Thompson was away on business, a band of terrorists descended on his plantation and burnt his home to the ground. His library and the records of a life-time's work curled into the tropic sky in a column of black smoke. But although Thompson rebuilt his home and continued his work as best he could, his cup of bitterness was not yet full.

Rumours began to spread saying that the American had recovered a fortune from the sacred well, the gold alone being worth more than 500,000 dollars. Eventually the rumour reached the ears of officials of the Mexican government and it took little time for them to decide that half a million dollars was a great deal of money. The government thereupon seized the Chichen Itza plantation until such time as Thompson could pay up more than half a million pesos.

Edward Thompson could truly claim to have been the first man ever to see the bottom of the well of the rain god and return to tell the tale. Nevertheless, it was the well which triumphed in the end. When, in 1933, he published his account of his discoveries, Thompson was still fighting to regain his home and his beloved Chichen Itza. But he met with little success, and two years later he was dead.

# Epilogue

THE treasures of Ur, Tutankhamen, Pompeii, Sutton Hoo, and Chichen Itza—these were some of archaeology's gilded moments. The newspapers of the world made them into nine-day wonders, spotlighting places and people of which the public had never heard before. Archaeologists are truly grateful for these sensational discoveries, for through the media of the press, radio, and television more and more people are becoming interested in a subject which before seemed reserved only for the dusty minds of bearded pedants.

But it would be wrong to jump to the conclusion that archaeology is really only a glorified treasure-hunt. To the archaeologist every discovery, however small, constitutes a great moment, provided that it adds something to our knowledge of man's past. The object today is to learn how our ancestors lived, and not merely to find new specimens to grace museum cases. A tiny fragment of pottery can tell as much as the discovery of a complete vessel, and a single battered coin in the right context can be much more valuable than a handful of gold recklessly torn from the earth. Traces of the foundation of a squalid hut in a ploughed field where no man is known to have lived can be of far greater importance than a heap of attractive relics from a site whose history is already well known.

Does this mean that modern archaeologists are not interested in making sensational discoveries, that they do not thrill at the sight of gold? Some will vow that this is so, claiming that there is not an ounce of the treasure-hunter's blood in their veins. But we must hope that they are deluding themselves, for such a person could hardly be human, and a man devoid of humanity, human weaknesses, or an understanding of human nature is unlikely to become a great archaeologist.